# Handicap[ Trainers

## IN SEARCH OF
## THE LONG SHOT WINNER

John Whitaker

© John Whitaker, 1990
LIBERTY PUBLISHING COMPANY
Deerfield Beach, Florida

Published by:
**Liberty Publishing Company, Inc.**
440 South Federal Highway
Deerfield Beach, Florida  33441


ISBN 0-89709-184-1

Manufactured USA

To the Pros—

The Trainers
who
Make it Happen!

# Contents

# Publisher's Note

*Handicapping Trainers* is a factual account of the author's trek through other ways and means, from, "Lord, where do I begin?" to, "Eureka! I found it!"

Why the author set out to do it is explained, of course. However, it should be noted that when this decision was made, he was already a successful handicapper, not someone in research or in computers with an idea for a new twist. Specifically, a working knowledge of relevant and meaningless racing information was brought to the research bench for closer examination...not the other way around.

For most serious racing fans, the study of trainers and their patterns will be useful in either of two ways: As an improvement to an existing handicapping method, or as a means of developing a personal list of "spot plays" for potential boxcar payoffs. The author goes one step further by presenting a unique way to capitalize on this newfound knowledge and shows how to bet accordingly.

Regardless of how the idea of handicapping trainers is applied, the author has clearly distinguished himself as *the* expert in this field. By following the author's lead, as outlined in this book, you will be given a running start on mastering an important aspect of horse racing -- and an entirely new way of looking at this exciting sport.

# Foreword

For years, trainer handicapping has been a jealously guarded secret of a select few. These few were willing to go to the exhausting trouble of searching out how certain trainers kept zipping home at 20 and 30-to-1, year after year. It was not easy getting this information. It still isn't, and that's why, even now, most handicappers are not privy to this level of knowledge.

Statistics are all over the place. They're cheap and easy to gather. Everybody has them; that is, everybody who is serious about being successful at the race track. Statistics have a value and, in most cases, are well worth the asking price. Don't ignore the fact that statistics have severe limitations, often overrun by handicappers in search of definite and easy answers to complex questions. Push the numbers too far and one discovers that no less than six horses will win today's race. Generally, statistics can answer "yes" or "no," but not "when" or "how." For when and how, one needs to search beyond the numbers.

How often have you heard that you can beat a race, but you can't beat the races? This omniscient speaker is everybody's bad news. A tip sheet grows from his shirt pocket. In one hand he holds a beer and the track program, and in the other, a hot dog with the mustard about to drip onto his shirt. A knowing, contented smile is always on his face because he has no worries at the track. He is comfortable, having long since come to terms with his lot. He's quick to tell you he is only there for the sport. A winner? No.

Actually, he is repeating something he heard that was confirmed by the results of his own failing attempt to "beat the races." How serious this attempt was is beside the point. He accepts his failure.

The best of professionals are fully aware of the uncertainties they face in every race. Even at one-to-nine, a horse is still a horse, half crazy in many ways. He'll throw his jockey at the bell just for fun. He'll stumble or fall, duck the shadow of a bird or plane, get bumped, pinched back, blocked, or fail for any or all of a dozen other reasons. One-to-nine is no guarantee.

These professionals also know there are many different ways to become a successful handicapper. Each way calls for it's own unique formula. The particular formula chosen is often dictated by the amount of time one can spend on the matter. Whatever the choice for whatever reason, when one finds a winning formula, the most common cause of failure is lack of discipline. It is often difficult to overcome, and it is *always* a problem when there are doubts about the formula.

This book describes the details of one winning approach. Furthermore, it presents such a clear and logical case that discipline should not become a problem. The uncertainty and hesitation (and downright fear) present in the line to the ticket window will pass away. *Handicapping Trainers* offers a method unlike anything you've seen before.

Race examples are described in detail and are representative of a much larger group. They are single incidents selected for their clarity to illustrate a particular point. The dozens of others that could have been detailed differ only in names, dates and places. There is no point padding this work with descriptions of like events. Read the examples carefully. The data is accurate. The realities are simple. I hope I've left them that way.

John Whitaker

# CHAPTER ONE

# Background

# Background

It was my misfortune to win a $316 daily double on my third day at the track on August 5, 1957.

Three days before I had been driving south on Route 9 from Lake George, wondering why all the traffic, when a blue uniform in the middle of the road demanded a left turn.

"But, I want to go to Albany!"

Several blasts of his whistle and vigorous waving convinced me to turn left or be shot. Fortunately, he couldn't hear my response as this left turn trapped me in a motorized queue all the way to the Saratoga parking lot. Then, what the hell? I'd never seen a horse race. It might be interesting.

The word "misfortune" was used recalling the few years following that first discovery of where all this easy money had been hiding. Three hundred and sixteen dollars, just like that! And I didn't even know what a furlong was. That was the least of my ignorance. It wasn't long before I lost my shirt, to say the least. Not a fond recollection. Eventually, I learned a few things and, in 1961, actually broke even. It was a good time to begin easing away.

The next thirteen years had nothing to do with racing. It was a prosperous time, and it was a circumstance similar to my first arrival at Saratoga that found me wandering into Calder Race Course during that fledgling track's fourth summer. It had been a long time; so long, it actually felt good to be there. Like remembering the fun of kindergarten but forgetting the unhappy times.

The names on the program meant nothing after all those years. It was enough to stroll, enjoying the sights and sounds and that fragrance found nowhere else in the world.

It took several hours to discover the group on the second floor west. A placard on the wall announced that Chuck Berndt conducted live seminars in this place every day through the first six or seven races. I stopped to listen and it is from this point, in this place, I began to learn the realities of racing. Very shortly I would begin a study of them.

Chuck Berndt drew me back to Calder again and again. His learned and personable manner was my first inkling that racing was a profession, as serious and meritorious as teaching, engineering or aerospace. If one were to take it on as a life's work with any hope of success, there were studies to be suffered, dues to be paid, and lumps to heal. Success, by any standard was there, but not for the desultory, the casual, the ignorant and undisciplined. It was not there for me, as I was.

I began to look ahead to a wonderful time, going back to school to a subject that intrigued and baffled brilliant minds for centuries. There was no lack of intellect. They were all being brilliant about something else, leaving racing for a pastime or avocation. "Sure, my pizza place is the busiest in the state. When I have time, I try to do brain surgery." This made about the same sense.

Chuck's approach was not a direct assault on which horse would win the race. For the hundred or so that camped at his feet every day, he labored to help them make a more intelligent bet, explaining the positives and negatives and why each applied today and not yesterday. He was a brilliant man with a tremendous knowledge of racing. It was a pleasure to listen and gratifying to learn. Along the way, I read everything possible. I don't remember making any bets during this time, but if so, they were the $2 variety, having nothing to do with wisdom. I was not ready for betting.

A year with Chuck went quickly and while I did not take up everything he proposed, he set me on the right path, teaching me what to study and how. From his criteria for an intelligent bet, it was a very short hop to a parallel study of what I call, the *the elements of a winning performance.* Andrew Beyer's *Picking*

*Winners* became one of my favorite books for it's simple logic regarding speed. Carrying his proposal several steps further gave me the credits needed for graduation in the fall of 1975.

The following two years of Speed Handicapping were the busiest and most financially rewarding of my life. I made my own par time charts every 3 months, along with track variants of incredible precision. My partner, Jimmy, was "Cash." I was "Horse." Together, we made a considerable dent in a lot of pocketbooks. After all, *somebody* had to lose that money.

It has been necessary to make you acquainted with this timeframe, when I handicapped horses and races, because *during* this period, the first seeds of *Handicapping Trainers* began to root, along with something else, something you'll recognize. It happened to me again and again, one of the most frustrating experiences encountered at a race track.

How many times have you labored hours over the *Form* and identified a horse that would have to drop dead to lose this race? You're out at the track, get your money down, and here it comes, leading by three into the stretch, streaking for the wire. Suddenly, from nowhere, blazing faster, is another animal that passes yours and goes on to score. You look down at your *Racing Form* to reexamine the winners credentials, and you were right the first time. No way! Impossible! How could anybody bet a horse looking *that* bad in his last two races? Four months ago... up in class... showing a pair of mediocre 3f b works... How? Still, there it was, on the board, paying $42.60. Many bettors agreed with you. No way!

Familiar? Let's take this scene a little bit further, to see at least one person making his way to the cashier's window for a payoff in four, maybe five figures. This person began setting this thing up some time ago. This person trained the winner and knew his (her) animal to be the superior force today. Unfortunately, at your expense, today was the day chosen to prove it. Your horse had all the right numbers. Every student of form agreed. By all conventional handicapping criteria there is no way this particular horse should have won. Your selection was the best horse but it was trashed.

Now, the worst part of this scenario has not yet happened, but it's about to. It begins when we shrug our shoulders, and ends when we turn back to our paper, chalking this experience up to that nebulous but prevalent, racing luck. Too bad.

Many, many times this scene swallowed my money. However, before chalking it up to racing luck, I did one more little thing, almost absent-mindedly. I glanced at the name of the trainer.

Months passed. It happened again and again. Slowly, through the mire of fudge I think with, I realized the same names were coming up, over and over; Lou Goldfine, Frank Merrill, Joe Pierce, William Knuck, Brian Webb, Art Warner, and others. It wasn't long before a race would be "passed" because one of these trainers had an entry that looked terrible. They were not handicappable! If I hadn't retreated from racing for several years, I might never have discovered the orchestration that went into some of those races; and I might have continued to make the same mistakes, accepting racing luck as a reasonable explanation.

I say, making the same mistakes. That's not quite right. We were making good money, handicapping horses and races. Those strange races presented little more than a frustration, a stumbling block after which we continued doing the things that worked for us, that kept the cash coming in.

There's an observation to be made here, to be recalled at a later time in this book. It has to do with that *continued* part. In handicapping horses and races, there is never any letup. There's never an easy time when you are caught up. You never get to lay back and coast. The decision-making process is ongoing from the time you get the paper, up to post time. You are continually examining conditions and sifting data. Does the horse look good? Is he sweating too much? Is he taking money on the board? Is he blowing out okay on the backstretch? Are the owners dressed for picture-taking? Do you have a bet, or not?

The race is off and in minutes you either win, or you lose whatever you bet. To recover that loss you have to duplicate that exact process again and again. One race is over. The next one begins, bringing all the same demands, questions and anxieties. There's no coasting; no resting. You're either in or out. If you're in, the pressure is on. To relax the pressure, you have to get out. There's no other way. Twenty years will pass and there will be no relaxing this routine.

In the fall of '76 I lost my partner, Cash, and in the weeks that followed, learned something about myself that wasn't going to do me any good. I had no idea how much Jimmy was needed until he was gone, forcing me to face how incredibly tight I am with a buck. No Diamond Jim here. I may have dreamed about letting it ride, but I choked on the words.

The past year and a half had been so good. The problem didn't exist because Jimmy was taking care of it for me. All I had to do was pick out the betting opportunities; two, maybe three a day; follow the action to a minute or so before post and then make the decision to go or pass. If it was go, Jimmy left his seat to do *his* thing, which was make the bet; $300 to win. Cash handled all the money and we settled up once or twice a month.

When Jimmy was gone, I learned what an incredible feat this was. Get up from the seat and walk to a line in front of the window. Check the program number. Go into a pocket for $300 in cash, step up to the window and hand it over to a perfect stranger for no other reason than a belief that the chosen horse would get to the wire before any of the other ten or eleven. All that money! Just hand it over for a thin ticket. I couldn't. Getting out of my seat was like having the priest there as the cell door opens. Walking to the line in front of the window was the last mile. It wasn't a window, it was a green door.

I couldn't make the bet. From the moment all the right elements were in place for a bet, a black cloud picked me out of the crowd and hung. A hundred objections to this whole charade came instantly to mind; too many reasons why my horse would lose. By the time I got to the green door, I *knew* there were easier pickin's in the next race. I returned to my seat without making the bet. I don't like to remember the times the horse that *didn't* get bet won the race.

It wasn't always like that. Most of the time I won the struggle and got the money down, but not always the whole $300. Without Jimmy, my income took a serious loss. I continued to make money, but not nearly as much as in partnership. You'd think it would be simple to replace somebody handling the money. I didn't find it so.

I continued alone into the following year but the constant pressure of finding the right bet along with getting the money down, which never got any easier, was a large part of my reason for quitting in April of 1977.

As for the other part, I had seen Seattle Slew set the Hialeah track record for 7 furlongs in prep for the upcoming Flamingo; which he also won by an incredible margin. No horse in the world would beat him in the Kentucky Derby. He was awesome. Daydreaming onward, I imagined the odds would be around one-to-three in this event. Too bad there isn't a way to get a price on him, for here was the answer to every horseplayer's dream. I knew what horse would win the race; I just *knew*! Then again, so did everybody else. If only there was a way...

What if a person... a corporation... no, it's too big for that. What if a *government* bet $50 million with bookmakers all around the country and then, at race time, tied up all the $50 and $100 betting windows, spreading another $2 million *on all the other horses* in the race...? What a story. What a *movie*!

I was bitten. I loved the idea. This was in the days *before* you could bet and cash any amount at the same window. I needed to write this movie, to get away from racing for a while; out from under the pressure. Writing this script was the perfect out and I took it. Racing wasn't going anywhere. It would still be there when I was ready again. Nothing could take away what had been learned. Racing would be my retirement plan.

I checked in at the Holiday Motel across from Hialeah and buried myself for the next six weeks writing a screenplay, "The Hayday Conspiracy." My par time charts were neglected; track variants fell behind and concentrated on my quest to get 15-to-1 on Seattle Slew in the Kentucky Derby. It was great being out of racing, relieved of that pressure.

After the screenplay, other things took my attention but racing was always somewhere on the edge of my thoughts. Someday I'd go back. Someday I'd find another partner and go back. It was too good to miss.

The next seven years are many other stories that have no relevance here, until the day in 1985 when I became tired of living many other stories. Perhaps it was time to go back to those sounds and smells that had been so good to me, that I really loved and would love more if only I could learn to loosen up the bucks.

The timing seemed right and I began putting together those things I would need; track history, charts and variants. Several times a week I made non-betting trips to the track to rekindle a few fires, resharpen a few senses dulled by many years of absence. It felt very good to be getting back.

I hadn't found a partner and decided to give it another try on my own, imagining time had somehow matured me enough to handle it. I'd keep my eye open for a Jimmy, but meanwhile...

My beginning was small and it went well. Time would be needed to recover past momentum. This "doing" part was necessary and soon everything fell into place. I had no problem betting $20's and $30's and thought to ease back to the heavier level. Winning more than losing indicated it was time to pick up the pace.

Then, in September something happened. You already know. I had the right horse and felt lucky to get 3-to-1. Again... leading into the stretch and, looking good... then, from out of the pack...

Looking down at the *Form*; no way! A second-time-starter named Crimson Anvil... no way! $69.00 to win. Then, an absent-minded habit made me glance at the trainer's name, "William Knuck!" WILLIAM KNUCK! He was doing this to me *ten years ago*! This was like a ghost laughing out of the past, "Got you again, sucker! Ha!"

He was still bringing horses home from nowhere.

The house fell on me. I'd like to say, "That wasn't necessary. I don't need a house to fall on me." Obviously, I needed exactly that. At that moment I no longer wanted the 3-to-1 runner that was obvious to everyone. I wanted that $69 horse William Knuck came up with. Before getting too deep into the old ways, it would pay me to rethink the entire situation. How in hell do you handicap a $69 horse? You don't really.

Knuck had pulled this off many times. I should be handicapping William Knuck! Where can I get a *Form* that will tell me the past performance of the trainer, not the horse?

This was the turning point in my approach to racing, the time when speed charts and all the lessons on conventional handicapping were put aside to go in search of William Knuck and *how* he put over that second-time-starter for $69.

There were to be many second thoughts as I looked around for a familiar point from which to begin. It was a wasteland, a desert, barren of any organized quantity of data needed to take the next step. I didn't even know what was needed.

# CHAPTER TWO
# The Logic

# The Logic

Who calls the tunes around the shed row, the owner? Most know a lot about money but too little about conditioning a thoroughbred; nor do many have the time. What about the jockeys? Riding six or seven a day, how can they keep abreast of the running style and present condition of each one? Often, there is a language problem and in the saddling shed, it's the trainer who instructs the jockey, not the other way around. A competent jockey follows those instructions if he wants another mount from that man.

The trainer is the *only* one with all the answers regarding the horse, so who is better equipped to determine the outcome of the race, or rather, the precise part his horse will attempt to play in it?

There was a time I got the word directly from the trainer. "It's a GO, today."

Privy to such inside knowledge I didn't hesitate making a large bet. Later, the trainer reeled off five very good reasons *why* our horse ran seventh (none of which cast the slightest shadow on his competence). I also experienced the reverse of this in the '76 Black Helen at Hialeah. "Yes Dear Maggy" was the only bet that day but when I heard, "Not today, friend; been having a lot of trouble with her legs," I cut the bet from $300 to $100.

Maggy won, of course, at 11 to 1. That earful of inside information cost exactly $2,200 and left me wondering for the first time, how to distinguish between three possibilities:

1)  Honest error in judgment
2)  Incompetence
3)  Deception

With very few exceptions, most trainers I know are good hard-working people who care about their animals. When it's a GO, they really *believe* they have a chance, and that's fine, but I needed a positive answer to, "Can the trainer get the job done?" Does he or she have a *history* of getting the job done under these conditions? Being a nice fella is great, but that's not a ticket I can cash. Putting money down, I needed to *know* if he or she can get the horse home in front when the odds-makers say, "No way." Who cares at 3 to 5?

When you have the details, the past performance of trainers reads the same as the past performance of horses. Those records tell of ability, competence and probability today. The only problem is, while the *Daily Racing Form* offers the past performance of the horse, nowhere can you find a detailed performance record of the one who pulls the strings.

Trainers, like the rest of us, follow normal inclinations toward pleasure and away from pain. If it feels good, they want more. If it works, try it again. If it works WELL, a behavior pattern may be tailored to maximize the pleasure. To a horse trainer, winning as planned is the best feeling in his world. It's his evidence of worth and final proof of personal success. Everything else is merely the result of that success. Again and again, the trainer will try with everything contributing to past success and avoid those things that, in his experience identify with failure.

The methods and patterns of Competent Trainers vary greatly; often opposing one another. Still, each in his own way will reach his goal. It is the purpose of *Handicapping Trainers* to use *history* to learn *definitely* who can do what, when and how?

It is a fact that some trainers *will* and some *will not* try to win with a horse that is:

a. SHIPPING in from another area of racing.
b. Coming back from a LAYOFF.
c. A First-Time-Starter.
d. On TURF for the first time.
e. Not near the top of his form.

The point of this work is to define a step-by-step method of learning precisely *who will* and *who will not*, and under *what conditions* will a trainer try with one, and not with another.

This information was not available in any book or package that could be read or examined reasonably. It did not exist in collected form of any kind. It had to be extracted bit by bit over several years and in a given form for which there were no parameters. It had to be sorted and analyzed over and over until the chaff was finally sifted away. The entire case for handicapping trainers rests on the results from information provided by this data.

With any study of this type, conclusions cannot be drawn from only a few samples. While the minimum number of samples required for reasonable conclusion will vary, it is certain the greater the number of samples, the more accurate will be the conclusion regarding probability.

It is important to emphasize the word "probability." When a trainer fails in a particular effort ten times in a row, it can not be CONCLUDED he will fail in the eleventh attempt. It *can* be concluded that his probability of success with number eleven is very small and is, as such, a very bad bet. Anybody who knowingly makes a bad bet of this type certainly deserves to lose.

Argue the question of probability further -- that each failure tends to increase the odds on the next attempt, that the law of averages will eventually turn up a success and probably at a big price. This can be true, but consider:

a.  To those who understand statistics, this isn't a sound explanation to the problem. Each race is totally independent of the next.

b.  Money is tied up that can be put to better use.

c.  Unless the trainer has proven to be competent in this particular endeavor (and it's our business to find this out BEFORE making our bet) he will lose, lose, lose -- while the price goes up, up, up. When he realizes he is not going to win at this level, he will drop the horse in class to get the win. Down in class means down in price and, while the entry may win, the resulting payoff may not be sufficient to recover the investment in his previous attempts.

Success, as we need to define it is not winning races, it's winning money. It's winning at the right price. The *right price* can only be one that consistently recovers all previous losses and shows a generous profit on top.

Another key word here is "consistently." If they run enough horses, all trainers will win races; some will win at some big prices because the law of averages is at work in this area, but unpredictably so.

Success is finding the trainer who has a HISTORY of getting a particular job done over and over. Consistency. All will try and most will have some success, but only a very few are able to succeed again and again. Researching their individual histories we will discover WHO these very few are long before anybody else catches on.

Accounting shows the normal cost of racing a horse runs between ten and twenty thousand dollars a year, depending on the class of the animal. Examine the upper right hand corner of *Daily Racing Form* past performances, where it lists "lifetime" earnings. Count the number of six-year-old horses that have yet to win thirty thousand dollars. Where is the money coming from, the money that keeps these horses racing?

It was mentioned earlier that a few seeds of *Handicapping Trainers* were planted back in the mid 1970's, but the constant pressure of handicapping horses and races left no time for most of those seeds to germinate; most, not all. One seed that managed to survive was planted by Neal Winick, then a prominent member of the noted family of trainers. Neal trained for many owners, among them, the late Mirabel Blum.

It could be seen that several of Neal's claimed horses were quickly run back, paying some great prices. So, I worked backwards through my papers, making a chart of ALL his claims with the result of their first and second races after the claim. It was quite a long list, but when I'd taken it back far enough, I was not as impressed as I thought I'd be. His performance appeared mediocre at best.

At the time, Jimmy and I fooled around with the list for a while, trying to corner *something* but it wasn't until I separated the claims *by owner* that Neal's stock shot off the board. He had some successes for Mrs. Blum but nothing to be excited about. However, almost every horse he claimed for Patti Mullady came right back, still in jail*, with a big price for win or place. There was no denying the figures.

"The next Winick claim for Patti Mullady is going to get our money, it doesn't matter who it's running against." It seemed the only way to go. He had demonstrated he knew what he was doing for that owner. It was equally obvious he had done all the handicapping necessary to know where to enter the horse, after he worked whatever magic the horse required. To second-guess him at this point would defeat the theory of this new awareness.

The day before Gulfstream closed in '76, the chance came. "Saint Cambridge," a nice turf mare, going up in class. The bet was automatic and I recall what a great feeling it was, being able to make a reasonable bet after SOMEONE ELSE (Winick) had done all the work. Had I a casual acquaintanceship with Mr.

---

*See Glossary.

Winick and asked him what his chances were, would he have told me? Could I believe him, if he did? After all, why should he go to the trouble of setting this up for a decent price, then hand it out to me, so I could tell my friends and they could tell theirs? Does that make sense? Would YOU give out this information?

I didn't have to ask Mr. Winick. I had researched his history and the facts were clear enough. He could have told me she had a broken leg, I still would have bet the horse.

Saint Cambridge finished second at 6 to 1. We never bet second. Jimmy had watched the race with binoculars. "It's not over yet," he announced with a hopeful glint.

Sure enough. Up went the "Objection" sign and Saint Cambridge gave me two "firsts" that day. 1) the first bet I ever made based on research of a trainer's history, and 2) the first time a disqualification put *my horse on top.*

The arrangements trainers have with owners are as varied as politicians' opinions, and knowing Mirabel Blum was not one to skimp on her thoroughbreds, I can only conclude the deal Winick had with Patti Mullady gave him more latitude for his selections.

There was a different feeling to winning that money; a piece of cake!

There was another seed, but I'm not revealing the names because this situation borders on collusion and one of the trainers is still active.

The 4th, 7th and 10th were Calder's trifecta races. Going back in my papers, I noticed that two particular trainers had a very high frequency rate as two of those three top finishers. A closer examination showed that, invariably, one entry was high on the selectors' lists and the other would be a longshot. I could almost hear one say to the other, "Listen, I've got a sleeper ready to run big. What have you got that can finish in the money?"

Look for: Trainers "A" and "B" with horses in the same trifecta race; one favored and the other, a long price.

The bet:   A $2 trifecta boxing A, B and all.

That combination came up 10 times after we got on to it. We won on 4; the smallest over $600. and the largest, $2,100.

The experience with Neal Winick's claims and the Trifecta Twins were my first with handicapping trainers; i.e., finding a professional who can *prove* he knows what he's doing, then letting him do my handicapping for me simply by entering his horse under a particular set of conditions.

I'd felt lucky to have discovered those two situations. It never occurred to me to drop what I was doing and search out *other* professionals doing the same thing.  I was too busy.

CHAPTER THREE

# Beyond the "Normal Routine"

# Beyond the "Normal Routine"

The weeks that followed Crimson Anvil are lost to any comprehensible description. William Knuck had driven the last nail into a big red sign that said, "Trainers ARE Doing Things!" But the sign didn't say, "what" or "how," much less, "when?" A journey began for which there would be no route, map or chart to point the way. Every step was new -- there was no picture. It was a puzzle turned upside down. The rules were to be made as I went, to be broken time and again, and discarded when they lost worth. The information needed did not exist *anywhere* in clusters of more than seven words or numbers. Answers were sought to questions that were in bits and pieces like everything else. How was I to get at it and extract it?

A handicapper of horses might better understand if asked, "Will you take this *Racing Form* I'm holding and handicap the Belmont card for me?" "Sure. Let me see the paper," he might say. "Of course, but first I have to pass it through this shredder...like...so. There. Now, the Belmont card, please."

Shortcuts were not appropriate. I was giving up a successful operation to pursue an idea with no clear definition. To give less than a total effort would be ridiculous. There could be no omissions because they were marginal or skipovers because the horse ran last, and who cares about a horse that ran last? It had to be done right and up to that time I never endured *anything* that made such demands on my discipline. I could taste that $69 horse as if it were on my plate. That event had been real and, if with enough effort, there was no doubt I could find out how it happened.

My first step was to define what to look for.

It seemed reasonable to go back through my library of *Racing Forms* to learn what William Knuck had done with other second-time-starters. Could there be anything in that history to tip me to his intentions with Crimson Anvil? While at it, I'd make a note of Knuck's first-time-starters. And what about Joe Pierce and the others I'd been wary of? How they handled these situations had to be considered also.

Hell, why limit my search to only a dozen trainers? Why not look up *everybody's* 1st and 2nd-time-starters? What about the 3rd-time-starters and the two-year-olds? What about the turf runners the 1st and 2nd time, and horses coming back from a layoff, and horses dropping in class or going up in class; trying a route the first time; the second; switching jockeys, and distances and tracks? More and more. There seemed no end to avenues to search and each new one doubled the previous work load. With only twenty-four hours in each day, it was becoming doubtful that I'd ever make another bet.

The pile of *Racing Forms* threatened from the corner. Did I really want to go on with this? Handicapping horses and races hadn't been all that bad. I'd be giving up any income for a while. There would be no time for the track or the rigors of conventional handicapping. My mental approach was terrible because patience hadn't played a winning hand in my whole life. Often, I inclined toward slipshod and this new idea was giving me a fit. There was no point in beginning unless it was done right and it looked like a hell of a lot of work. The pile sat for days before the first paper was opened.

There would be no return to my former ways... ever. This new bit was in my teeth. Running with it or choking on it were the only choices. Withdrawing to some insane place where only tunnel-vision was practical, work continued until bedtime. Tomorrow was just a word. Today, there was only this paper that had to be finished. Complete this paper and quit if you want. Well, maybe I can do one more; but that'll be *it*. Just one more.

After two months of this distorted existence, I was back at the beginning. So much data was contradictive; a morass defying all attempts at anything reasonable. I'd gone after it all; and *all* was proving much too much. I backed off to make cuts. Forget about getting it all... settle for *half*. It was a while before I found my way again.

Recalling that my search was for POSITIVE answers to PARTICULAR questions, there was a need to eliminate all elements that could not be precisely defined. A horse going up from $14,000 to $16,000 was offering very little distinction, as was the horse stretching out from a mile and a sixteenth to a mile-and-an-eighth. Then I recalled a line from one of the Calder Seminars, something about horses taking turns beating each other. Just then, suddenly, everything fell into place.

All those horses involved in the "normal routine of racing" (i.e., similar horses taking turns beating each other under similar conditions and distances for nine or ten months a year) had to be eliminated. Then, if they were lucky, they'd go off to the farm for a couple of months, grazing under untroubled skies. Then, back to training, and back to the races. The cycle would be complete.

Eliminate horses involved in the normal routine when distinguishing one from the other was impossible. But, aaahhh, Eureka! *Outside* that normal routine, there were many situations permitting very positive distinctions to be made. For example: In a field of eleven competing, examination would show that nine fall into that "normal routine" category. One is coming back from a three months layoff on the farm (and this is the first race) and another was claimed two weeks ago, out for the first time for the new ownership (and trainer). We have two horses racing in positively identifiable situations outside that normal routine.

What can be learned here? Nine horses will show us little we can put our finger on with certainty. Two will give us *a piece* of something positive. The first two questions are: "Will Trainer A bring his horse back running, after three months away, or will he give him a race or two for conditioning?" Does Trainer B know what he's doing when he claims a horse?

The result of the race offers nothing conclusive but it gives us a few bits of very specific information in addition to presenting a few more questions. Neither horse came close to winning. We need to watch them the next time out.

It's common knowledge, though not outwardly advertised, that some trainers will be trying and some will not, with horses they bring back from a Layoff; with a First-Time-Starter; on the Turf the first time; with a Shipper; etc., etc. -- under all those identifiable situations outside the normal routine of racing. Our questions have a very reasonable order designed to bring us one step at a time toward *any* definite information that may be available. More often than not, nothing can be concluded. But then, you can't reasonably hope to win every race anyway. Many times the answers permit very definite conclusions and this, in the end, is what we're after. Follow the sequence.

- Who are the trainers who will try?

- Who are the trainers who will not try?

- Of those who *do* try, which trainers have a history of succeeding?

- Which trainers have a record of repeated failures?

Will trainer A bring his horse back running from the three-month layoff? Look at the result of the race. His horse ran seventh. Still, we don't know if the horse was breezing, or was actually trying and failed. If the horse finished second or third, our question is probably answered (this trainer *will* try) and we can forget about his next race. Because he ran seventh, so we still don't know. But the next time this horse runs he will add to our knowledge. He will be running his second race after a three month layoff and this, too, is a very identifiable situation. Will he try this time? Again, this race is only important to follow if the horse finished fourth or worse in the first race back from the layoff. In this second race, he finishes second.

What do we know? We've seen a horse come back from a three- month layoff and run seventh. We don't know if he tried. We saw him come back in his next race and run second. We can assume he was trying to win. That's all we know. We don't know if the horse's second race was run any harder than the first contest. Finish position means very little.

What we have just learned means nothing when viewed separately, or if we disconnect these events from the trainer. We *have* a valuable bit of information, but if we are to realize it's full potential, it must be placed alongside a dozen or more *similar* events brought about by this same trainer. How did he handle all of them? Only then can we hope to see a PATTERN emerge, if there *is* a pattern. Too often, there is none. More precisely, 95% of the time, there is none.

# CHAPTER FOUR
# Getting Organized

# Getting Organized

After discovering what to look for, the next step was to define each of the pieces, to identify and describe precisely what would constitute situations outside the normal routine of racing. The list that follows took several months to evolve. Much effort was wasted on situations that eventually proved unwieldy or of too little value, such as dropdowns. I didn't want to track anything that *reduces* the probable odds, like winners that repeat. I wanted to catch their *first win*. After the first win they belong to the public and the professional selectors.

There is one situation in racing that is unique. It causes a trainer and/or owner to publicly challenge the competency of another trainer. It happens in the claiming process. In this instance, a claim is to seize ownership of a horse -- to appropriate a horse by lawful means -- to take ownership of a horse without negotiation.

Claiming races are the principal means of leveling competition, making it very risky for the owner of a superior horse to enter it against cheaper company just to make off with the purse. Any licensed person may claim the superior horse for the listed price. The majority of races in this country are claiming races offering unique opportunities to the superior horseman.

It is natural for some of us to be prepossessed regarding what we call "ours." My car is faster than your car. My dog is smarter than your dog. My pop can lick your pop. To horsemen, this translates, "My horse is worth a lot more than I paid for it."

To prove what a sharp deal he made, he enters a horse he claimed for $25,000 in a $35,000 race*, hoping for one or both of two things:

1) Verification of the sharp deal when the horse wins at this higher level, or

2) At least one other licensed person will see potential in the horse and claim it away for $35,000, providing a $10,000 profit whether the horse wins or not.

Frequently, evidence will suggest a lousy deal. The horse couldn't come close at $35,000 and nobody put in a claim slip. Something must have gone wrong. Another try. The loss is repeated. Dropping the horse back to $30,000. proves no help. Any lower drop will lose money and if money is lost, the deal wasn't quite that sharp. No trainer wants to advertise a bad deal, so the horse will continue to be raced over its head, and this story goes on and on.

Prepossession (or prejudice) is evidence of incompetence. The sharp horseman knows the intrinsic value of any animal he claims or purchases. He also has a good idea of the degree to which his care and training can improve the animal. When this is accomplished, he knows exactly where to enter his horse, and at what level of competition he can successfully challenge.

This is one of the people we're looking for and finding him requires an approach different from any of the others. For this reason, claiming records should be kept apart from all the others.

To consider claiming a horse, a trainer must first believe the present owner/trainer has not been able to get the best of what the animal has to offer. He must believe the horse is potentially worth more than the price for which it is being entered. He must believe the performance of the horse can be improved to a profitable degree.

By claiming the horse, a trainer tells the previous management and the entire racing world that he can do a better job with the horse. It's easy to see how this can become personal.

Personalities aside, we need to know if the claiming trainer knows what he's doing -- and the only way we can find out is to study the history of his previous claims. Did he succeed with them? How many? To what degree? Does he show an overall profit in this activity? Can his successes and/or failures be attributed to one or more factors we can see before the race?

All trainers are often wrong. We're looking for those who are wrong least often and can show a profit. To find them, we need certain information about *every* claim made, and a card file, 4" x 6", indexed by trainer's name seemed the most practical way of collecting it. For every claim, it was was necessary to record:

1) Trainer name
2) Horse name
3) New Owner for whom the claim was made.
4) Date of claim
5) Claim race
6) Claim track
7) Claim price
8) Where the horse finished in the claim race

The above describes the claim itself. Recording the name of the owner and trainer from whom the horse was claimed required a doubling of search efforts with 95% of this time wasted on losers. It was necessary to learn who the winning 5% were, then go back and collect the "previous owner/trainer" information if it was relevant. This proved to be a practical decision.

For my purposes, not always the trainer's, success could only be achieved if the trainer was able to win one of the first three races after the claim at odds great enough to show a profit if an automatic $2 bet was made on each of these races. It follows, if the new trainer wins with the horse the first race after the claim (while still in jail) the betting profit potential is the greatest. The potential of the second and third races after the claim depends on many factors we need not go into now, lest we lose sight of the point -- that of searching out a *history* of success. We need to look at a trainer's record with at least FIVE claimed horses to begin evaluating his expertise.

That he won or lost is not enough. Details not available in statistical compilations can turn an apparent loser into great profit and this fact will remain lost to anyone not able to examine such details. If the trainer wins with the horse the first time out after the claim, what more can he tell you in subsequent races? It follows, if the horse wins the second race after the claim, the question of expertise is likewise answered and tracking any race beyond this (for this horse) becomes unnecessary. The following information on each of the first three races was recorded after every claim or, until the first win:

1) Interval (days between the claim and 1st race)
2) Race date
3) Race number
4) Race track
5) Class of race (claiming price or allowance purse)
6) Closing odds
7) Finish position
8) Jockey's name

It was noted earlier that 95% of all data collected is wasted effort...the details on losers. Much time and effort is saved if, first, the *winners* are identified, and then the additional details of race distance, surface, post position, sex, etc., are added if/when they are needed.

A color-code on the card with a magic marker proved to be a good idea. A solid orange stripe along the top of the card indicated the trainer won either the first or second race after the claim. A broken orange and black line said the trainer won the third race after the claim. A solid black meant the trainer failed to win any of the first three races after the claim.

Looking down at this drawer full of cards, it was easy to spot a batch of orange, pull it out, and see who contributed what. A batch of black had much to say, also. Recording claims is the quickest and most certain way to get a line on successful trainers. A lifetime annuity can be achieved by setting up and maintaining this file. One need not go any deeper.

Going deeper, where desire, time and energy permit, is accomplished by tracking (in addition to claims) the many other situations that can be precisely identified, that require no thought or decision or ambivalence. My personal list appears here and since I required the same detailed information on all of them (different from what I needed for claims), they can be dealt with collectively.

FTS    A First Time Starter, three-years-old or older.

2TS    A Second Time Starter, three-years-old or older. Most of the second time runners were tracked only if they ran poorly (4th or worse) the first time. If they finished 3rd the first time, obviously, the question, "Will he try?" is answered. That he tried and failed is also obvious.

FTS2  Same as above, but a two-year-old.

2TS2  Again, a two-year-old 2nd Time Starter.

It's reasonable to assume that every trainer will be trying third time with any situation, if the horse is sound.

L1-3  A horse coming back from a Layoff of 1 to 3 months.

L4-8  A horse coming back from a Layoff of 4 to 8 months.

L9    A horse coming back from any Layoff of 9 months or more.

2L1-3 This is the horse's 2nd race after a 1-3 month Layoff

2L4-8   The horse's 2nd race after a 4-8 month Layoff.

2L9     2nd race after a Layoff of 9 months or more.

S       Shipper. From another region of racing. This code is used by itself or in conjunction with any other code except FTS or FTS2.

2S      2nd race after Shipping.

FTT     First Time on the Turf.

2TT     2nd race on the Turf.

Rt7     Route to 7 furlongs, for tracks that run 7 furlong reces. These runners are generally sprinters to begin with or middle distance runners with a lot of early speed. The trainer's objective here is to set up a price and beat a field of 6 furlong horses. The sprinter is given one or more races of a mile or more that he is not trying to win. The trainer wants to build the horse's stamina, increase his lung capacity a bit. When the trainer feels this is accomplished, he searches for a 7 furlong race with many 6 furlong runners entered. The plan being, while the 6 furlong runners are backing up in the final eighth, the one or more route races will have given his entry just enough extra stamina to prevail in that final furlong. The race *must* be 7 furlongs, not 6f or 6 1/2. The route race preceeding today's 7 furlongs must have been run in the past three weeks, or the beneficial effects on stamina will dissipate.

StR     Sprint to Route. While many knowledgeable handicappers may disagree here, my studies suggest that a normal sprinter will not usually win around two turns. Preparations will vary with each trainer. Many try but few can pull it off repeatedly.

FBK Fastback. This is an infrequent situation, but it almost always generates a big price. Generally there is something wrong with the horse, something minor. It's not serious enough to take the horse out of training (which can be expensive), but the risk of further complication is strong if the animal is pushed too hard before the problem is corrected. The past performances will show light racing, approximately once a month (24 to 36 days) for at least two months, but hopefully for three or more. None of these races will show a winning effort (sixth or worse, generally). Today, the horse is back after only 7 to 12 days. He's BACK FAST. The indication is, the trainer feels the problem is corrected. You can expect the horse to be all out today. This is an excellent situation in the hands of a few trainers. Many try, but...

Needless to say, these items will keep a normal man up to his hips for quite a while. A little imagination can provide others. These situations (I call them INDEX) will be dealt with in this book. Some are described in greater detail further on.

After *defining* these situations, the next step was the madness of marking (coding), to go back to my oldest *Racing Form* and examine each horse in every race, to see if any were racing under one or more of these special situations. Those that were, needed to be marked with a code of some kind and the abbreviations shown above were used.

The past performances for the sixth race at Calder display this simple marking system. Nothing esoteric. Once you work with them, the codes become obvious.

**6 CALDER** (6 FURLONGS)

**6 FURLONGS. (1.08⅘) MAIDEN CLAIMING. Purse $6,000. 2-year-old maiden fillies. Weight: 120 lbs. Claiming price $20,000; for each $1,000 to $18,000 allow 2 lbs.**

**Kolorado Kris** 2TS — B. f. 2, by Sezyou—Collection Plate, by Cyclotron — $20,000 Br.—Heath Bonnie M (Fla) Tr.—Erb Dave — 120 — Lifetime 1 0 0 0 $90 — 1985 1 M 0 0 $90
Own.—Laurel Mar Farm
19Dec85- 8Crc fst 6f :23 47 1.13⅘ ⒻMd 50000 3 7 5² 85¾ 9¹⁴ 918¾ Russ M L 120 21.10 64-18 Miss Toasty 118¹ Dance On Snow 116¹ Starlite Art 120²½ Outrun 11
LATEST WORKOUTS Dec 16 Crc 3f fst :37 bg Dec 10 Crc 5f fst 1:04⅘ b Dec 6 Crc 5f fst 1:06 b Dec 2 Crc 5f fst 1:04⅘ b

**Ray's Jet** FTS — Dk. b. or br. f. 2, by Ray's Word—Happy Weaver, by Loom — $18,000 Br.—Davis & Rank (Ky) Tr.—Estevez Manuel A — 116 — Lifetime 0 0 0 0 — 1985 0 M 0 0
Own.—Block & Estevez
LATEST WORKOUTS Nov 17 Crc 5f fst 1:03 b Nov 9 Crc 4f fst :50⅕ b Nov 2 Crc 5f fst 1:03 b

**Manhattan Queen** L3½ — Ch. f. 2, by Effervescing—Manhattan Doll, by Wig Out — $20,000 Br.—Meadowbrook Farm Inc (Fla) Tr.—Masters Kenneth — 120 — Lifetime 4 0 1 3 $4,710 — 1985 4 M 1 3 $4,710
Own.—Lacroix Barbara
4Sep85- 6Crc fst 6f :22⅕ :46⅕ 1:13⅘ ⒻMd 25000 1 3 1¹ 2hd 1hd 36½ Baltazar C b 118 *.70 75-15 CrimsonAnvil118³SheliaGaye118³½ManhttnQueen118nk Weakened 10
7Aug85- 6Crc fst 6f :22⅕ :46⅗ 1:13⅘ ⒻMd 30000 8 2 1² 1hd 22½ 2⁴ Baltazar C b 118 *3.00 78-15 Grotona 114⁴ ManhattanQueen118³½FashionJet114nk Second best 12
25Jly85- 6Crc fst 6f :22⅗ :46⅗ 1:14⅗ ⒻMd 25000 7 5 42½ 52¾ 3¹ 3¹ Baltazar C b 117 3.10 78-16 SweetSunset117¹Cynthi'sMoment117noMnhttnQuen117²½ Rallied 11
28Mar85- 3Hia fst 3f :22⅗ :34⅗ ⒻMd Sp Wt 2 1 42½ 3³ Smith A Jr 117 8.50 86-11 Sweet Puddles 117hd Babbsie 117³ ManhattanQueen117nk Rallied 8
LATEST WORKOUTS Dec 14 Crc 3f fst :37 bg Dec 7 Crc 6f fst 1:16⅗ b Nov 30 Crc 5f fst 1:02 b Nov 24 Crc 4f fst :49 b

**Memorette** FTS — B. f. 2, by Taylor's Falls—Memorare, by Tell — $18,000 Br.—Gallagher J H (Ky) Tr.—Broic Danny — 116 — Lifetime 0 0 0 0 — 1985 0 M 0 0
Own.—Gaylor A
LATEST WORKOUTS Dec 28 Crc 4f fst :50⅗ bg Dec 10 Crc 4f fst :50⅗ bg Nov 26 Crc 4f fst :50 b Nov 21 Crc 5f fst 1:04⅗ b

**Golden Streaker** — Ch. f. 2, by Tonkaton—Annie's Heels, by Tumble Turbie — $18,000 Br.—Cole B (Ky) Tr.—Hemmerick Anthony J — 111⁵ — Lifetime 3 0 0 0 $180 — 1985 3 M 0 0 $180
Own.—Grassymeade Stable
24Dec85- 6Crc fst 6f :22⅗ :47⅕ 1:14⅘ ⒻMd 16000 11 2 5³ 54½ 69½ 710½ Baltazar C 126 6.80 66-18 Our Tonka Toy 120¹½BendsQueen120⁴½BethsBracelet115¹½ Evenly 12
27Nov85- 4Crc fst 6f :22⅗ :46⅗ 1:13⅘ ⒻMd 20000 8 2 41½ 54½ 5¹¹ 6¹³ Baltazar C 119 82.90 69-20 Sudden Dash 119⁴½ Pearlofgreatprice 119³½ Seething 119½ Tired 9
18Nov85- 4Crc fst 6f :22⅗ :47 1:15 ⒻMd 25000 8 9 107½ 1111⁵ 1015 913½ Drawdy T 119 52.40 62-22 Proveolot119²½DawnofTime119nkBlueandBeutiful119nk No factor 12
LATEST WORKOUTS Dec 21 Crc 4f fst :53 b Nov 25 Crc 4f fst :53 b Nov 16 Crc 4f fst :50 b Nov 11 Crc 5f sly 1:05 b

**Bends Queen** — Dk. b. or br. f. 2, by Bends Me Mind—White Eyed Lady, by Cabildo — $18,000 Br.—Pennbrook Farm (Ky) Tr.—Mendez Jose A — 116 — Lifetime 2 0 1 0 $1,140 — 1985 2 M 1 0 $1,140
Own.—Garazi S
24Dec85- 6Crc fst 6f :22⅗ :47⅕ 1:14⅘ ⒻMd 16000 6 5 3² 2¹ 22½ 21½ Soto S B 120 *2.90 75-18 Our Tonka Toy120¹½BendsQueen120⁴½BethsBracelet115¹½ Gamely 12
11Dec85- 2Crc fst 6f :22⅗ :46⅗ 1:14 ⒻMd 18000 8 7 63½ 5⁶ 4⁹ 48½ Suckie M C⁵ 111 8.20 73-18 Perlofgretprice120⁴½Ms.HppyHour120¹½ScrppyDrling116² Rallied 12
LATEST WORKOUTS Dec 21 Hia 5f fst 1:03 b Dec 5 Crc 5f sly 1:05 b Nov 30 Crc 6f fst 1:19 b Nov 23 Crc 5f sly 1:04⅗ bg

**Irish Slang** 2L4½ — Ch. f. 2, by Irish Ruler—Coin A Phrase, by Cavan — $20,000 Br.—Bloodstock M & M (Fla) Tr.—Sanchez Juan — 115⁵ — Lifetime 3 0 0 1 $1,130 — 1985 3 M 0 1 $1,130
Own.—Cowan Marjorie & I M
18Dec85- 4Crc fst 6f :22⅗ :46⅗ 1:13⅘ ⒻMd 20000 1 3 5² 54½ 44½ 46½ Suckie M C⁵ 111 5.10 76-15 Fastcean 120³ Matte Finish 120¹½ Silky G. 120¹½ Evenly 10
2Aug85- 4Crc fst 6f :22⅗ :47⅗ 1:14⅗ ⒻMd 20000 3 8 4¹ 32½ 43½ 37¾ Soto S B 118 2.90 71-19 Mrs. Bumble 118⁴½ Mi Fi 114³ Irish Slang 118²½ Lacked fin.bid 12
25Jly85- 6Crc fst 6f :22⅗ :46⅗ 1:14⅗ ⒻMd 25000 11 3 76¾ 65½ 55½ 64½ Birklin A M⁷ 110 13.50 74-16 SweetSunset117¹Cynthi'sMoment117noMnhttnQuen117²½ Outrun 11
LATEST WORKOUTS Dec 16 Crc 4f fst :52⅗ bg Dec 11 Crc 6f fst 1:17 b Dec 5 Crc 5f sly 1:06⅗ b Nov 29 Crc 4f fst :52 b

**Rapid Rio** 2L2 — B. f. 2, by Rio Carmelo—Commie, by T V Commercial — $18,000 Br.—John Mac Farm (Ky) Tr.—Bucci Art — 116 — Lifetime 3 0 0 0 $85 — 1985 3 M 0 0 $85 — Turf 1 0 0 0
Own.—Tiffany Stable
9Dec85- 1Crc fst 1⁷⁰ :50⅗ 1:16⅗ 1:47⅘ ⒻMd 35000 3 7 63½ 7¹¹ 8²⁹ 8³⁸ Castaneda K 120 34.70 33-17 Raspberry Beret 120⁷ Darby Del 111²½ Turvei! 120½ Outrun 8
11Oct85- 6Del fm 1 Ⓣ:49⅕ 1:14⅗ 1:42⅗ ⒻMd Sp Wt 2 2 7⁷ 79½ 8¹⁸ 7¹⁷ Melendez J H 120 60.60 46-35 Sly Silk 120nk Bashful Star 120⁴½ Majestic Pleasure 120² Brief ft. 12
25Sep85- 5Del fst 6f :22⅗ :46⅗ 1:13⅕ ⒻMd Sp Wt 5 7 87½ 8⁹ 46½ 611½ Melendez J H 120 56.30 63-23 Zane My Love 120⁶ BashfulStar120noE.T.'sFantasy120½ No factor 12
LATEST WORKOUTS Dec 28 Hia 3f fst :37⅗ b ●Dec 19 Hia 6f fst 1:17⅗ b

**Emerald Rain** — B. f. 2, by Baldski—Silver Rain, by Roan Rocket — $18,000 Br.—Maxwell R (Fla) Tr.—Domino Carl J — 116 — Lifetime 3 0 0 0 $170 — 1985 3 M 0 0 $170
Own.—Maxwell R
18Dec85- 6Crc fst 6f :22⅗ :46⅗ 1:13⅘ ⒻMd 25000 3 7 6⁴ 915 1119 1018 Vergara O 120 28.10 66-15 Spiriting 120¹½ To Reason Why 120½ Gentle Margie 120⁷ Outrun 12
4Dec85- 6Crc sly 6f :22⅗ :46⅗ 1:13⅘ ⒻMd Sp Wt 1 9 6⁷ 5⁷ 1011 1011½ Vergara O 119 25.70 71-13 Drama Prospect 114²½ Talski 119¹ Dance Reality 119¹½ Outrun 11
17Aug85- 7RD gd 5½f :22⅗ :47 1:07⅗ ⒻMd Sp Wt 12 7 8⁷ 1013 1015 1019½ Zook D J 120 38.60 57-26 Final Regret 120⁴ Gold N' Arizona 120½ Fly Feliou 115¹½ 12
LATEST WORKOUTS Dec 14 Crc 5f fst 1:03 b ●Nov 28 Crc 6f fst 1:18⅗ b ●Nov 19 Crc 5f sly 1:02⅗ b Nov 6 Crc 5f fst 1:03 b

**Flight North** FTS — Ch. f. 2, by Sunny North—Twin Star, by Wishing Star — $20,000 Br.—Baguell N (Fla) Tr.—Lyons Larry — 120 — Lifetime 0 0 0 0 — 1985 0 M 0 0
Own.—Baguell & Lyons
LATEST WORKOUTS Dec 11 Crc 4f fst :50⅗ bg Dec 5 Crc 4f sly :50 b Nov 30 Crc 3f fst :38 bg Nov 15 Crc 3f fst :38 b

**Pretty Tangy** 2TS — Ch. f. 2, by Olantengy—Pretty Chipper, by Royal Note — $20,000 Br.—Gray Betty & C W (Fla) Tr.—Mettz Arthur E — 120 — Lifetime 1 0 0 0 $90 — 1985 1 M 0 0 $90
Own.—Gray C W
19Dec85- 8Crc fst 6f :23 :47 1:13⅘ ⒻMd 50000 2 10 108½ 1117 1126 1133¾ Valdivieso H A 120 49.00 49-18 Miss Toasty 118¹ Dance On Snow 116¹ Starlite Art 120²½ Outrun 11
LATEST WORKOUTS Dec 10 Crc 5f fst 1:04⅗ b Nov 30 Crc 3f fst :38 b Nov 25 Crc 5f fst 1:04⅗ b Nov 18 Crc 3f fst :38⅗ bg

**Lady's Dignity** S — Gr. f. 2, by Silent Dignity—Gold Sash, by Sovereign Edition — $20,000 Br.—Alexander Helen (Ky) Tr.—Crupi James J — 115⁵ — Lifetime 5 0 1 0 $2,250 — 1985 5 M 1 0 $2,250
Own.—Sharenow Ethel
26Nov85- 4Med sly 6f :22⅘ :46⅘ 1:14⅘ ⒻMd 16000 8 7 8¹⁰ 6¹² 48½ 2⁶ McCauley W H b 117 3.00 63-29 Miss Caitlin 112⁶ Lady's Dignity 117²½ Doctor's Lass 117¾ Rallied 10
20Nov85- 1Med fst 6f :23⅗ :47⅘ 1:13⅘ ⒻMd 18000 12 9 84½ 75½ 46½ 58¾ McCauley W H b 115 3.80 66-20 MissDrumBeat117noProspector'sDnce117⁷½SyltPlin117¹ Wide trn 12
21Oct85- 3Med fst 6f :23 :47 1:12 ⒻMd 28000 6 3 4¹ 3³ 46½ 6¹⁵ Madrid A Jr 113 11.90 67-23 Invalid 115⁶½ Yo Madrid 117² Say It Plain 107²½ Tired 9
27Jun85- 4Mth fst 5f :23 :46⅘ :59⅘ ⒻMd 25000 9 4 3½ 33½ 55½ 7¹² Antley C W 117 *1.80 76-19 BiddinOnABeauty117¹TulipsAreUp117¾HollyHgley117³ Thru early 9
17Apr85- 4Hia fst 3f :22 :33⅘ ⒻMd Sp Wt 7 7 44½ 44½ Fires E 117 5.90 91-04 Joey Blue 117¹ Miss Avionce 117¹½ Curious Lady 117² Evenly 10
LATEST WORKOUTS Dec 27 Hia 5f fst 1:01⅗ b Dec 20 Hia 4f fst :50 b Nov 9 Med 3f fst :37 bg

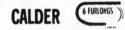

"Manhattan Queen" L3 1/2: Coming back from a LAYOFF of three and one-half months.

"Irish Slang" 2L4: This is the horse's second race after a LAYOFF of four months (approximately).

"Lady's Dignity" S: SHIPPER, from another region of racing.

In this procedure, every horse is examined to see if any INDEX notation is appropriate. Every horse, every race, every day, for as many tracks as you care (or have time) to follow.

The order of procedures for handicapping trainers is:

1) Decide exactly *what* situations you will research and give them precise definition (parameters).

2) Identify and code (mark in the paper) *all* horses racing under one or more of the chosen situations (INDEX).

3) Extract the *necessary pieces* of information on the coded horses to a paper form, which can be put in alphabetical order, indexed on the trainer's name or enter this coded data into a computer.* What are the necessary pieces of information? These parameters also must be *created*. There are no established guidelines for this kind of investigation.

4) Transfer the extracted and "alphabetized" data to the individual trainer's record.

5) Analyze the trainer's record for success patterns.

6) Tell everybody about what you found. Perhaps you should write a book!

---

*NOTE: This early portion of *Handicapping Trainers* will ignore the fact that computers exist and describe the operations as they must be done by hand. More on computers will be written later. These items will vary with the individual searcher, based on what he or she considers important.

The elements listed here are certainly not the *only* worthy considerations. Successful handicappers see many things differently on their way to the cashier's window. The elements chosen were those that worked best for me. They had been part of a successful operation and I saw no reason to abandon them, just because my handicapping was taking on new form.

When these procedures are performed on a day-to-day basis, keeping up is not a problem. It becomes something else when you are at the beginning of your task, looking at a pile of *Racing Forms* that can stretch backward for six months, or even a year, and you *know* you'll not be able to even begin the job of *listing* your data until every horse in that pile has been properly coded. It's easy to see why handicapping trainers is not a widely used approach. It can be a masochistic undertaking.

## CHAPTER FIVE
# The Necessary Pieces

# The Necessary Pieces

Every successful handicapper has long decided what bits of information are necessary to a particular approach to winning. Before any success, there was probably a great deal of shuffling and switching things around until a particular combination of parameters reversed the flow of cash. Once this reversal was a-chieved, great care was taken from that point onward that no *new* piece of information be allowed to disrupt the rate and direction of that flow.

This does not imply the learning process is halted. There is always the hope of IMPROVING things. From time to time, a new item will be taken on to see if the cash flow "in" can be increased but this is always done with great care to see there is no backsliding from what had been satisfactory.

Most of the choices recommended in this book are obvious. If this list is questioned at all, it will more likely be for has been left out. There are, indeed, many others. The "left out" items that have been tested and rejected are too numerous to detail. Unfortunately, it will be neccessary for you to explore other avenues on your own. Some may, in fact, prove successful, depending upon the special circumstances of your local racing circuit.

The following is what I record for every horse that races under one or more of the INDEX described above, regardless of where the horse finishes in the race. We want to know *who can not*, as well as *who can*.

If post positions were awarded based on the alphabetical arrangement of trainer's last names, this would be a much easier goose to cook.  As it is, we must go down our list of coded runners (see the last example) from Erb to Estavez, to Masters, Broic, Sanchez, Bucci, Lyons, Metz and Crupi.  Each of these trainers is giving us a bit of information in this race and we have to find a way to get it from the paper, to some form we can sort easily.  If we pull Erb's file to enter what happened to "Kolorado Kris;" return it, and pull the Estavez file to enter "Ray's Jet," we will spend two-thirds of our time thumbing through our file.  Nothing is getting done while we're thumbing.

One reasonable solution places an extra step between the *Racing Form* and individual trainer's file, but it was the best that could be devised. Alphabetical divider pages were put in a loose-leaf binder, then a few blank forms were added between each of these pages (see page of names beginning with "S"). Then, working down the horses in the 6th at Calder, the loose- leaf binder would be opened to the "E's" and "Erb, Dave (or whatever had to be recorded for Kolorado Kris)" would be entered. Then, because the "E's" would still be needed, on the line directly underneath, "Estavez, Manuel" (and whatever is to be noted for Ray's Jet) would be recorded.  Now, flipping to the "M's" notations for "Masters, Kenneth" (and the data on Manhattan Queen) would be entered.  Flipping back to the "B's" to enter "Broic, Danny" and the data on Memorette would be next.

This process continued until *all* Index Runners in the *Racing Form* had been entered in the loose-leaf book.  From these alphabetical pages, the transfer of the data to the individual trainer's record, which was done about once a week, was simplified.

| 1 TRAINER | 2 DATE | 3 RA | 4 TRK | 5 DIST | 6 INDEX | 7 NAME | 8 AGE CL | 9 LAST RACED | 10 WORKOUTS | 11 ODDS | 12 FIN | 13 JOCKEY |
|---|---|---|---|---|---|---|---|---|---|---|---|---|
| Sanchez, Gregory | 6-18 | 1 | Occ | 5 | ETS 2 | Happy Hasty | 3x25 | — | | 6-15 | 11 | Acquel |
| Smith, William | 6-18 | 4 | Occ | 5 | ETS 2 | Dudes Struttin | 2x05 | — | | 6-51 | 9 | Davis |
| Stuckey, Alex | 6-21 | 1 | Occ | 6 | L-4 | Royal Conch | 4y 12-15 FebTam-1½ | | | 10-38 | 9 | Sirius |
| Sanchez, Juan | 6-19 | 10 | Occ | 6½ | L-751 | Portanto | 5c10 JanTuSaT5sd1 | 15'1b, 21b, 46 | | 5-9 | 8 | A-Teter |
| Stauchfield, Charles | 6-21 | 1 | Occ | 6 | ETS | Not Apparent | 3x12 | — | | 6-2 | 7 | Lee |
| Smith, William | 6-21 | 2 | Occ | 6 | L-4 | O, Tonka Toy | 3x22 2YFebGP3str | 46, 5b, 5b, 46 | | 8-5 | 7 | Dominguez |
| Simms, Philip | 6-21 | 4 | Occ | 5 | ETS | Balla, Cat | 3m5w | — | | 8-21 | 10 | Velooble |
| Smith, William | 6-21 | 4 | Occ | 5 | ETS 2 | Irish Tunk | 3m5w | — | | 10-37 | 11 | Brien |
| Schandt, Hilma | 6-10 | 3 | Occ | 5 | ETS iz | Second Prophecy | 2m5w | — | | 6-12 | 5 | Astoga |
| Stone, Joseph | 6-22 | 4 | Occ | 6 | ETS | Penny Weight | 3m5w | — | | 8-24 | 6 | Hotman |
| Ortiz, Ronald | 6-22 | 7 | Occ | 6 | L-6 | Queen's Justice | 3mw2 2Dec CR2 3-17 | 46, 5bg, 5b, 46 | | 8-12 | 5 | Hozeand |
| Simms, Phillip | 6-23 | 1 | Occ | 5 | ETS 2 | Julie's Blossom | 2x15 | | | 8-15 | 9 | Castaned |
| Ortiz, Ronald | 6-25 | 5 | Occ | 5 | ETS 2 | Batcha's Joe | 2x35 | — | | 8-21 | 6 | Hozeanck |
| Selden, Stuart | 6-25 | 7 | Occ | 6 | L-6 | Stu's Honey | 3x35 9Dec CR2 5-34 | 46, 5bg | | 12-37 | 7 | Caveruck |
| Simms, Phillip | 6-26 | 1 | Occ | 5 | ETS 2 | Chill Bump | 2x18 | — | | 6-1 | 1 | Castaneo |
| Summons, John | 6-26 | 4 | Occ | 6 | L-3 | Win A Gallant | 4y 11-6 3MayCR2 12-23 | 46, 4b, 2½maj, 24b 13-61 | | 15-61 | 9 | Squaztin |
| Sanders, Gregory | 6-26 | 5 | Occ | 82 | BOTL-3 | Ankle Blur Eye | 5c 14 15Dec CR2 L-5 | — | | 4-5½ | 1 | Lester |
| Simms, Philip | 8-27 | 2 | Occ | 5 | ETS 2 | Match Stick | 2x18 | — | | 16-6 | 5 | Castaneo |
| Startts, Charles | 6-27 | 4 | Occ | 5 | ETS 2 | Above Gossip | 2x25 | — | | 10-13 | 7 | Pierce |
| Sannico, Jess | 6-27 | 6 | Occ | 5 | ETS 2 | Doctor's Pirate | 2x22 | — | | 16-63 | 5 | Duracte |
| Starts, Charles | 6-28 | 4 | Occ | 5 | ETS 2 | Doc's Embrace | 3m5w | — | | 16-15 | 1 | Acquel |
| Schandt, Hilma | 6-28 | 8 | Occ | 6 | L-7 | Mezra/Cathy | 4mw2 4Jul CR2 5-34 | 5b, 5b2, 5bg, 46 | | 10-8 | 4 | Duracte |
| Sanchez, Gregory | 6-29 | 1 | Occ | 5 | ETS 2 | Johnnia | 2x25 | — | | 8-6 | 6 | Espan |
| Stone, Joseph | 6-29 | 1 | Occ | 5 | ETS 2 | Bay Brlwws | 2x25 | — | | 5-5 | 8 | Sinson |
| Smith, William | 6-29 | 5 | Occ | 7 | MASK | Medeval Eye | 4Jul 18Jul CR2 7-14 | — | | 5-2 | 1 | Brien |

This next process, creating the individual trainer's record, began by typing "Sanders, Gregory" at the upper-right of a blank sheet of paper. Now, every line of information in the loose-leaf book beginning with "Sanders, Gregory" would be typed on this page. The name in the loose-leaf book would then be crossed out with a yellow marker, to indicate the information had already been transferred to the Trainer's file.

With Gregory Sanders' individual record in the typewriter, the information on "Happy Hasty" on June 18 would be copied from the loose-leaf binder. While Sanders' record was still in the typewriter, it was easy enough to look down the list of names beginning with "S" (underneath), for any other Sanders' runners to be added. "Annie Blueeyes" on June 26 was added. No other Sanders' entries? His record was returned to the file; those two items marked yellow in the loose-leaf book; and then the record for "Smith, William" would be pulled. Repeat the above. Pull "Stuckey, Alex," and so on. By using the yellow marker after making the transfer, the same sheet in the loose-leaf book could be used until it was filled. A small thing; however...

So much for the "how?" Now we come to, "what?" The forms just described speak for themselves. It was necessary to record that on June 18 trainer Gregory Sanders ran a 2 year-old First Time Starter (FTS2) in the first race at Calder Race Course over a distance of 5 furlongs. If this race had been on the turf, distance would have been marked "5T". The class of this race for 2 year-olds was Maiden Claiming (x) for $20,000 (20). As a First Time Starter, "Happy Hasty" had no previous races and Sanders is showing *no* workouts in the *Racing Form*. The track program odds on "Happy Hasty" were 6 to 1 and they closed at 15 to 1. "Happy" finished 11th in that race and Acevedo was the jockey. A jockey apprentice allowance is also recorded when appropriate.

If this horse had a previous race, as did "Queen's Justice" on June 22, it would have been recorded that "Queen's Justice" last raced on December 2, and finished third in that race at odds of 17 to 1. "Queen's Justice" was given four workouts prior to today's race and the lack of any underlined number, as with "Portanto's" workouts June 19, tells us all these workouts were given within a period close enough to one another to make all of them relevant to preparation for today's race. The underlined numbers indicate "days prior to today." "Queen's Justice" last workout was a 6 furlong, breezing. The prior workout was 5 furlongs, breezing from the gate, then 5f b, and 4f b.

Subsequently, the ownership of the horse was included, an important step, but that does not appear at this time.

The inclusion of track program odds* that can be compared with the actual closing odds allowed the creation of a list of trainers whose entries were to be watched carefully if they were bet down, particularly if there was no obvious reason for this bet-down. Conversely, another list of Trainers was made whose entrys would take a fortune on the board and it didn't improve them an inch.

With this list, one would never be concerned that the choice would go to 40 to 1. You learn to *love* it.

This is all the information that will be recorded for each Index runner. The only changes made in two years are the dropping of several Index items that proved impractical or of too little potential, such as the "RPT3" for "Annie Blueeyes." RPT3 (Repeat 3) means the horse won it's last 2. Exotic bettors will find it useful. I'm no longer interested.

The coding for column #8 regarding the age of the horse and class of the race was changed once all the tracks in the East were researched, to better reflect that a "Non-Winner of 2 Allowance Races" at Calder is one thing; at Belmont, it's something quite different.

Each line of information constitutes a single entry on the trainer's record. A nine- or ten-race card at any track will offer

---

*NOTE: It is necessary to have the track program morning line odds for this purpose. The professional handicappers at the *Daily Racing Form* should be respected, but the need to prepare their lines so far in advance deprives them of early scratches and other benefits enjoyed by the track handicapper who makes the program selections.

approximately 50 lines of information on 35 different trainers. It's unbelievable how rapidly this data accumulates. Still, it took an accumulation of nearly seven months before my first dollar was bet, based on an analysis of each trainer's record. It was a day I'll never forget.

| DATE | RACE | TRK | DIST | INDEX 1 & 2 | HORSE NAME | AGE & CLASS | LAST RACED | WORKOUTS SINCE | ODDS | FIN | JOCKEY |
|---|---|---|---|---|---|---|---|---|---|---|---|
| 5/30 | 6 | Crc | 6 | L4 | Legal Legacy | 3c25 | 10JanGP9@35 | 194b / 0 | 10-9 | 7 | St.Leon |
| 5/31 | 3 | Crc | 5 | FTS2 | Eloquent Miss Rex | 2MSW | | | 8-10 | 3 | Hernandez |
| 5-31 | 9 | Crc | 7 | L9 | Cox's Miss | 3Stk | 23AugCrc1@1 | 6b,6b,5h,4b | 20-20 | 12 | Lester |
| 6/1 | 3 | Crc | 5 | FTS2 | Scottom | 2MSW | | | 10-42 | 7 | Arias |
| 6/1 | 4 | Crc | 6 | FTS | Desi Sue | 3MSW | | 0 | 8-2 | 8 | St.Leon |
| 6/4 | 3 | Crc | 5 | FTS2 | Court Quill | 2x20 | | 0 | 8-11 | 1 | Velez, J. |
| 6/4 | 5 | Crc | 5 | FTS2 | Valid Awareness | 2x40 | | 0 | 5-2 | 2 | St.Leon |
| 6/5 | 1 | Crc | 6 | FTS | Isn't She Romantic | 3x10 | | 0 | 8-8 | 3 | Arias |
| 6/5 | 3 | Crc | 5 | FTS2 | Lucky Court | 2x15 | | 0 | 4-3 | 1 | Velez, J. |
| 6/5 | 6 | Crc | 8½ | FTS | Individual Effort | 3x25 | | 0 | 10-31 | 8 | Arias |
| 6/5 | 7 | Crc | 6 | FTS | Dusty Gal | 3MSW | | 0 | 8-16 | 4 | Cardone |
| 6/6 | 1 | Crc | 5 | FTS2 | Smart Court | 2x40 | | 0 | 3-3 | 1 | Pennisi |
| 6/6 | 2 | CRc | 5 | FTS2 | Blues Court | 2x25 | | 0 | 8-4 | 1 | Lester |
| 6/6 | 3 | Crc | 5 | FTS2 | Pleasure Court | 2x15 | | 0 | 3-2 | 2 | Arias |
| 6/7 | 1 | Crc | 6 | L7 | Rehearing | 8c7 | 2NovCrc6@2½ | 3b,4b,4b | 3-4 | 2 | St.Leon |
| 6/7 | 11 | Crc | 6 | L6 | What Intensity | 3c40 | 14DecAqu7@29 | 3b,25db,4b,3b | 10-4 | 6 | Velez, J. |
| 6/8 | 3 | Crc | 5 | FTS2 | Captivating Appeal | 2MSW | | 0 | 5-7 | 6 | Velez, J. |
| 6/11 | 6 | Crc | 6 | FTS | Timeless Winter | 3x40 | | 0 | 8-9 | 9 | Pennisi |

ROOT, Richard R.    Page 2

For some time, this page and the Alphabetizer Sheet have been given over to the computer. Data is entered directly from the coded paper and this Trainer's record resides permanently in the computer from where it can be easily searched with a few keystrokes.

CHAPTER SIX

# The Trainer's Record

# The Trainer's Record

It's difficult to say just how many samples of a situation are needed before we can start to draw conclusions, or how much evidence of a pattern be required before going into our pocket for a bet. Very few samples might lead us to a wrong conclusion; if we require too many, a lot of money can be left on the table (in addition to losing our discovery to the public). Experience suggests so far that each situation has to be examined as totally unique. No rules. No guarantees. As in handicapping horses, you end up making the best estimate possible with the information at hand.

Early in April, 1986, I believed enough data had been accumulated on enough trainers to begin an analysis of their records. Just getting this far was a tremendous boost to a morale that for too long had wisely refused to look at itself. I needed this time. Whether I found anything or not, reaching the time to begin looking, was a milestone. Beginning with the "A's"...

Abdale, Jose - Only two entries on this record.
Alexander, Frank - 21 entries - 8 wins, 1 place, 4 shows.

This record presented my first betting opportunity, and now you can see exactly what I saw on April 12. (Of course, you cannot have precisely the same vantage point after months of experience with it, but you'll see how it works. The concept may be strange, codes unfamiliar, and, in some cases, reasons for my choices might not be that clear. Still, you will undoubtedly see what I saw).

The following record of Frank Alexander is exactly as it appeared then. What is here is the basis for my conclusions.

Examine it carefully. Resist the urge to jump pages ahead to see what happened. Take whatever time you need to study the material. That you are reading this book testifies to some interest in the prospect of handicapping the trainer. Unravel this mystery yourself.

We're looking for WINNERS, trainers with a history of wins. There's something to be said for losers with a pattern, but it's not very exciting. Frank Alexander's eight wins from 21 dissimilar examples certainly screams out for closer examination. This fact is quickly grasped looking down the second column from the left -- the "Finish" column.

TRAINER:  Alexander, Frank

PAGE 1

| RACE DATE | RACE # | TRACK | DIST | INDEX #1 | INDEX #2 | HORSE NAME | AGE | CLASS | LAST RACE Date, Track, Finish, Odds | WORKOUTS Since Last Race w/Interval 1&2 | ODDS | FIN | JOCKEY |
|---|---|---|---|---|---|---|---|---|---|---|---|---|---|
| 11/30/85 | 3 | CRC | 7 | FTS2 | | MAGGIE GAYLORD | 2 | MSW | | -5B6,-5B,, | 2.00 | 3 | Vasquez |
| 12/19/85 | 7 | CRC | 8.5 | S | | ANNIE BLUEEYES | 4 | C20 | 11/25/85ANU8314.00 | -4B,-;, | 51.00 | 1 | Lester |
| 12/27/85 | 10 | CRC | 6 | L7 | | NAHEMA | 4 | NW2 | 05/11/85CRC297.00 | -4B6,-4B,, | 1.00 | 1 | Vasquez |
| 01/07/86 | 3 | CRC | 9T | L3 | I | DARBY LADY | 4 | NW2 | 10/21/85ENG11011.0 | -4B,-4B,5B,BB | 13.00 | 1 | Vasquez |
| 01/07/86 | 4 | CRC | 6 | FTS | | FANTASTIC ROBBER | 3 | MSW | | -5B,-4B6,6B6,5B | 14.00 | 1 | Vasquez |
| 01/08/86 | 8 | GP | 8T | L3 | | WATCH WORD | 5 | NW3 | 10/19/85CRC423.50 | -4B,-5H,5H,4B | 10.00 | 1 | Vasquez |
| 01/17/86 | 8 | GP | 7 | FTS | | MAKEESHA | 3 | MSW | | -4B6,-5B6,5B,5B6 | 3.00 | 3 | McCauley |
| 01/27/86 | 4 | GP | 7 | FTS | | SWEET SHERYL | 3 | MSW | | -5B,-4B6,5B,5B | 6.00 | 7 | McCauley |
| 01/29/86 | 8 | GP | 7 | FTS | | ENTERTAIN | 3 | MSW | | -4B6,-4B6,5B,4B | 8.00 | 3 | Vasquez |
| 02/06/86 | 6 | GP | 7 | FTS | | ETERNAL VOW | 3 | MSW | | -5B,-5B6,4B6,4B | 6.00 | 4 | Lester |
| 02/17/86 | 6 | GP | 7 | 2TS | | ETERNAL VOW | 3 | MSW | 02/06/86GP438.60 | -3H6,-;, | 5.00 | 1 | Lester |
| 02/26/86 | 8 | GP | 8.5T | L2 | | STRANAR | 4 | NW9 | 12/25/85CRC1026.00 | -4B,-5B,4H,5B | 6.00 | 6 | Lester |
| 03/01/86 | 3 | GP | 6 | FTS | | DOC CONNOR | 3 | MSW | | -4B,-4H,6B,5H | 12.00 | 12 | St. Leon |
| 03/06/86 | 9 | GP | 8T | L2 | | PURPLE COMET | 5 | NW5 | 01/21/86GP633.50 | -5H,-4H,6B,5H | 7.00 | 1 | St. Leon |
| 03/17/86 | 9 | HIA | 7 | L6 | | CHOCOLATE SWISS | S | STK | 09/22/86BW0201.00 | -5B,-4B,5H6,4B | 6.00 | 6 | Perret |
| 03/19/86 | 6 | HIA | 6 | L5 | S | NARROW ESCAPE | 3 | NW1 | 10/20/86BEL621.50 | -5B,-5B,5B,5B | 35.00 | 7 | Bailey |
| 03/29/86 | 8 | HIA | 8.5 | L2 | | DARBY LADY | 4 | NW3 | 01/21/86GP992.00 | -6B,5B,5B,5B | 15.00 | 3 | Riveria |
| 04/05/86 | 8 | HIA | 7 | L2 | | WATCH WORD | 5 | C45 | 02/10/86GP637.00 | -4B,34-4B6,5B, | 6.00 | 2 | Perret |
| 04/07/86 | 8 | HIA | 6 | L6 | S | KID COLIN | 3 | NW3 | 09/28/86BEL806.00 | -4B,-3H,5H,3H6 | 5.00 | 5 | Lester |
| 04/10/86 | 8 | HIA | 8.5T | 2L5 | | NARROW ESCAPE | 3 | X46 | 03/19/86HIA725.00 | | 3.00 | 1 | Perret |
| 04/12/86 | 4 | HIA | 6 | FTS | | COOL IT | 3 | MSW | | -4B6,-5B,4B6,5B | 8.00 | 8 | Squartin |

We see a Show finish on November 30, followed by five wins. The column to the left of Finish displays the Odds. Check the Closing Odds. This man has *something* going for him and, obviously, we're going to miss it all if we wait for his runners to take money on the board.

Finding the trainer with successes, checking the closing odds to see if these were all favorites, offering very little, is how to begin the analysis. His prices were impressive, so the next step would be to move left to the column that lists the INDEX his horses were running under, to see if any of these Index match up with 1's or 2's in the Finish column. Colored markers can be used to tag things you want to notice.

The above ends the preliminary search. If there are no matches, go on to the next trainer's record. If there *are* matches, a secondary search must begin, using Distance and Track Surface as the sort mechanisms. Owners come next, but not at this time.

To refresh your memory: FTS = First Time Starter; with a "2" added, the horse is a 2 year-old. 2TS = Second Time Starter. S = Shipper. L7 = Layoff of 7 months (coming back from). L3/I = Layoff of 3 months and an imported horse. All distance is expressed in furlongs. 8.5 is equal to one and one-sixteenth miles. A "T" added means the race was on the TURF.

Can you find one or more patterns in this trainer's data? If you can, describe what you will *look for* in Frank Alexander's future Index Runners.

Experience has also tells us to search *only one step beyond* the evidence of any pattern that appears profitable, and this search is generally for NEGATIVE information, the conditions within the pattern definitions under which the trainer fails often. In other words, when you find something good, try not to slice it too thin.

Now begin your search. On a separate piece of paper, try to write a brief summary (100 words or less) of Frank Alexander's activity, including what you will be looking for in his future Index Runners. See how your summary compares with the one that was written on April 12:

"ALEXANDER, Frank one for seven with FTS; three of seven in the money. His best performance is with the first start on dirt or turf after a layoff of 2 to 3 months. With this, he is winning three of six (all on the Turf) at odds of 13-1, 10-1 and 7-1. He finished second with another at 6-1 and third with another at 15-1. Record is uninspiring with Layoffs of 4 months or more. His 2nd best performance is with 2TS but very limited data."

"...best performance is with the first start on dirt or turf after a LAYOFF of 2 to 3 months." Granted, this is a limited amount of data, but it's as close to conclusive as we can hope to come to at this time. As mentioned earlier, wait too long and *everybody* will see it.

Coding today's races with the above analysis in mind, I could begin looking specifically for Frank Alexander's Index Runners and, in particular, for an "L2, L2.5, L3 or L3.5" and, if it's coming back to a TURF RACE, I could become emotional. I didn't have to wait too long.

Examining the past performances for the 8th race at Hialeah on April 15, I got that first tingle of excitement that precedes a long awaited event. Based on your own analysis of Frank Alexander's record, how does "OK Fine" look to you?

**8 HIALEAH** TURF 1 1-16 MILES HIALEAH START FINISH

**ABOUT 1 1/16 MILES. (Turf). (1.39⅘) ALLOWANCE. Purse $11,000 (Plus $1,000 FOA). 4-year-olds and upward which have not won a race other than Maiden, Claiming or Starter. Weight, 122 lbs. Non-winners of a race other than Claiming at a mile or over since February 15 allowed 3 lbs. Such a race since January 15, 5 lbs.**

**OK Fine** L 2 Dk. b. or br. c. 4, by J O Tobin—Fine Prospect, by Mr Prospector
Own.—Stonewall Farm Br.—Matthews Carla (Ky) Tr.—Alexander Frank A 1125
Lifetime 13 1 0 3 $16,470 | 1986 3 0 0 1 $2,080 | 1985 10 1 0 2 $14,390 | Turf 8 1 0 2 $12,820

| | | | | | | | | | | | | | | | | | | | |
|---|---|---|---|---|---|---|---|---|---|---|---|---|---|---|---|---|---|---|---|
| 13Feb86- 8GP | fm | *1 1/16 ⓣ | | | 1:45⅘ | Alw 16000 | 8 | 3 | 31½ | 54½ | 911 | 814 | St Leon G | b 122 | 4.80 | 66-18 | MasteroftheGme1124½Convergence117¾PointofOrder117no | Tired | 10 |
| 3Feb86- 7GP | fm | 1 1/16 ⓣ | :47 | 1:11⅘ | 1:43⅘ | Alw 16000 | 11 | 6 | 58 | 56½ | 913 | 67¾ | St Leon G | b 122 | 3.20 | 73-12 | Envol II 117¾ Shallow Diplomat 1222½ Convergence117hd | No rally | 12 |
| 20Jan86- 8GP | yl | *1 1/16 ⓣ | | | 1:49⅘ | Alw 16000 | 4 | 2 | 11 | 1½ | 1hd | 31¾ | St Leon G | b 122 | 8.10 | 57-39 | Raise A Beau 1221 Explosive Dancer 117¾ OK Fine1222 | Gave way | 10 |
| 31Dec85- 8Crc | fst | 7f | :22⅘ | :46 | 1:25⅗ | 3+Alw 11000 | 8 | 2 | 2no | 53½ | 89 | 711¾ | St Leon G | b 116 | 6.50 | 77-19 | Royal Christopher 1133¾ Mr. C. D. 113nk Wardlen 1161¾ | Tired | 9 |
| 3Dec85- 7Crc | fm | *1 1/16 ⓣ | | | 1:47⅗ | 3+Md Sp Wt | 1 | 1 | 11 | 11 | 14 | 14 | St Leon G | b 120 | *1.90 | 60-31 | OK Fine 1204 Endured 120½ Henri Matisse 1203½ | Ridden out | 8 |
| 18Nov85- 4Aqu | fst | 1 | :47 | 1:11⅗ | 1:36⅘ | 3+Md Sp Wt | 2 | 1 | 11 | 1½ | 2½ | 31½ | Graell A | b 120 | 9.50 | 81-13 | Muscovado 1201 Crafty Runner 120nk OK Fine 1202½ | Weakened | 10 |
| 8Nov85- 4Aqu | yl | 1 1/16 ⓣ | :49⅘ | 1:16⅕ | 1:49⅘ | 3+Md Sp Wt | 7 | 1 | 11½ | 12½ | 1hd | 43½ | Graell A | b 120 | 8.10 | 53-38 | The Tinkerman 1151½ Backstreet 1201½ Zoning Board 120¾ | Wide | 10 |
| 5Nov85- 5Med | fst | 1 1/16 | :48 | 1:13 | 1:46⅕ | 3+Md Sp Wt | 3 | 1 | 11 | 2½ | 32½ | 45 | Graell A | b 118 | 3.70 | 67-20 | Saavedra1182½[DH]Provnte'sEncore118nk NobleStlement1182½ | Tired | 8 |
| 20Oct85- 6Bel | fm | 1 1/16 [T] | :48 | 1:12⅕ | 1:45 | 3+Md Sp Wt | 4 | 2 | 42 | 32½ | 36½ | 37½ | Graell A | b 119 | 38.10 | 68-22 | Kyaera 119½ I'm A Knockout 1197 OK Fine 1121¾ | Hung | 8 |
| 20Jly85- 3Bel | fst | 7f | :23 | :46⅗ | 1:24⅗ | 3+Md Sp Wt | 2 | 6 | 52 | 67 | 718 | 727½ | Graell A | b 116 | 15.30 | 51-22 | Wicked Wike1163½CostConscious1161½GrittiPalace1162 | Fin.early | 8 |

LATEST WORKOUTS Apr 11 Crc 4f fst :50 b Apr 5 Crc 5f fst 1:02⅕ b Mar 29 GP 5f fst 1:01⅗ b Mar 23 GP 4f fst :49⅘ b

This race had me more hyped than any Christmas morn I can remember. It was here. All the work of the previous months was about to cross the bridge of theory. It was well hidden from the public eye, and it was coming down today.

Recall the times a long-price horse came in, and when you looked back at your *Racing Form*, you could *then* see how one or two things made it possible. I was now looking at my records and seeing those one or two things *before the race*. The clues could not be found in the *Racing Form*, or anywhere else. "OK Fine," laid off two months and coming back to the turf. Talk about tailor made...Merry Christmas!!

I took my friend C.T. Scott to Hialeah that day. He's a $2 bettor, but he believed me to the tune of 20 bucks. Making the bet, I was trembling with delight.

"OK Fine" lay close on the far turn where he took the lead and pulled away in the stretch to 3 1/2 lengths with all the authority of a practiced hand. I can't tell you how good it felt!

**EIGHTH RACE** **ABOUT 1 1/16 MILES.(Turf). (1.39⅘) ALLOWANCE. Purse $11,000 (Plus $1,800 FOA).**
**Hialeah Park** **4-year-olds and upward which have not won a race other than Maiden, Claiming or Starter. Weight, 122 lbs. Non-winners of a race other than Claiming at a mile or over**
**APRIL 15** **since February 15 allowed 3 lbs. Such a race snce January 15, 5 lbs.**
**Value of race $11,000; value to winner $6,600; second $1,980; third $1,210; fourth $550; balance of starters $110 each. Mutuel pool $42,599. Perfecta Pool $27,406. Trifecta Pool $36,883.**

| Last Raced | Horse | Eqt. | A. | Wt | PP | St | ¼ | ½ | ¾ | Str | Fin | Jockey | Odds $1 |
|---|---|---|---|---|---|---|---|---|---|---|---|---|---|
| 13Feb86 $^{8}$GP$^{8}$ | OK Fine | b | 4 | 117 | 3 | 2 | $2^{hd}$ | $3^{3}$ | $3^{6}$ | $1^{½}$ | $1^{3½}$ | Soto S B† | 9.10 |
| 5Apr86 $^{12}$Hia$^{8}$ | Timur Lank | | 4 | 117 | 4 | 4 | $4^{5}$ | $4^{4}$ | $4^{5}$ | $4^{5}$ | $2^{2½}$ | Terry J† | 25.10 |
| 8Apr86 $^{8}$Hia$^{2}$ | Pas De Cheval | | 6 | 117 | 2 | 1 | $3^{2½}$ | $2^{2½}$ | $1^{hd}$ | $2^{1}$ | $3^{3}$ | Hernandez C | 3.10 |
| 19Mar86 $^{8}$Hia$^{7}$ | Space Rider | | 4 | 117 | 5 | 3 | $1^{1½}$ | $1^{1½}$ | $2^{2½}$ | $3^{1½}$ | $4^{1½}$ | Velez J A Jr | 2.60 |
| 21Mar86 $^{7}$Hia$^{4}$ | Endured | b | 4 | 117 | 6 | 7 | $6^{½}$ | $6^{hd}$ | $5^{½}$ | $5^{½}$ | $5^{4}$ | Duarte J C | 5.80 |
| 3Apr86 $^{6}$Hia$^{1}$ | Trader Al | | 5 | 117 | 1 | 6 | $5^{hd}$ | $7^{4}$ | $6^{2½}$ | $6^{4}$ | $6^{1½}$ | Rivera M A | 4.60 |
| 7Apr86 $^{3}$Hia$^{1}$ | Windy City Son | b | 4 | 112 | 8 | 10 | $7^{5}$ | $5^{hd}$ | $7^{4}$ | $7^{4}$ | $7^{nk}$ | Lester R N$^{5}$ | 20.80 |
| 20Jan86 $^{8}$GP$^{6}$ | Alleged Affair | b | 4 | 117 | 10 | 9 | $9^{½}$ | $8^{½}$ | $8^{½}$ | $8^{1}$ | $8^{no}$ | Castaneda K | 9.10 |
| 27Mar86 $^{5}$Hia$^{1}$ | Raise The Dues | b | 4 | 112 | 7 | 5 | 10 | $9^{½}$ | $9^{1}$ | $9^{5}$ | $9^{7}$ | Suckie M C$^{5}$ | 11.00 |
| 1Apr86 $^{4}$Hia$^{10}$ | Viceless | b | 4 | 117 | 9 | 8 | $8^{hd}$ | 10 | 10 | 10 | 10 | Gonzalez M A | 43.80 |

**OFF AT 4:25 Start good, Won driving. Time, 1:43⅘ Course firm.**

| $2 Mutuel Prices: | | | |
|---|---|---|---|
| 3-OK FINE | 20.20 | 12.80 | 4.20 |
| 4-TIMUR LANK | | 24.60 | 7.00 |
| 2-PAS DE CHEVAL | | | 3.60 |

**.$2 PERFECTA 3-4 PAID $454.80. $2 TRIFECTA 3-4-2 PAID $1,128.00.**

**Dk. b. or br. c, by J O Tobin—Fine Prospect, by Mr Prospector. Trainer Alexander Frank A. Bred by Matthews Carla (Ky).**

OK FINE never far back, gained command in midstretch from the outside and then drew clear. TIMUR LANK raced forwardly, could not gain on the winner in the final eighth, but was best of the others. PAS DE CHEVAL prominent from the outset, gained command on the second turn, but weakened in midstretch. SPACE RIDER set the pace for six furlongs, then faltered in midstretch. ENDURED was forced into TRADER AL going into first turn.



There was something about winning this race that's hard to describe even today. Handicapping the trainer had worked, at 9 to 1. It was only a race. He got lucky. Everybody gets lucky. Even I get lucky. I wasn't buying any of that for an instant. It was written, preordained. It had to happen that way or all of history would be a meaningless chronicle of no value in learning about tomorrow. Luck? Not on your life!

At the time I found this thing in Alexander's record, I also came up with information on several other trainers; one of whom was Gregory Sanders. I didn't have as much data on him as on Alexander, but I had enough to write the following report:

> "SANDERS, Gregory    Gets in 1st or 2nd at big prices. Goes the second time out, generally."

Not much data, but what was there indicated a noticeable degree of competence. "Gets in 1st or 2nd at big prices." This was a flag. We're not interested in *anybody* who gets big prices. "Goes the 2nd time out, generally." We're looking for a "2L", a horse who is out for the second time after a Layoff of 'x' months and one that did not look very good the first time out.

"OK Fine" had won the 8th race; Gregory Sanders offered "De Jeau" in the 9th.

 HIALEAH

7 FURLONGS    (1.20½) ALLOWANCE. Purse $15,000 (Plus $2,000 FOA). 4-year-olds and upward which have not won $8,505 three times since September 15 other than Maiden, Claiming or Starter. Weight, 122 lbs. Non-winners of $10,000 since January 1 allowed 3 lbs. $8,600 since November 1, 5 lbs. $9,000 since October 1, 7 lbs. (Maiden, Claiming and Starter races not considered in allowances0

| De Jeau | 2L7 |
|---|---|

Back to the window for Gregory Sanders "2L7", second race after a Layoff of seven months that was something less than intimidating in the first race on March 29th.

**NINTH RACE**
## Hialeah Park
**APRIL 15**

**7 FURLONGS. (1.20⅗) ALLOWANCE. Purse $15,000 (Plus $2,000 FOA). 4-year-olds and upward which have not won $9,605 three times since September 15 other than Maiden, Claiming or Starter. Weight, 122 lbs. Non-winners of $10,000 since January 1 allowed 3 lbs. $9,600 since November 1, 5 lbs. $9,000 since October 1, 7 lbs. (Maiden, Claiming and Starter races not considered in allowances0**

**Value of race $15,000; value to winner $9,000; second $2,700; third $1,500; fourth $750; balance of starters $150 each. Mutuel pool $40,660. Perfecta Pool $28,458. Trifecta Pool $31,067.**

| Last Raced | Horse | Eqt. | A.Wt | PP | St | ¼ | ½ | Str | Fin | Jockey | Odds $1 |
|---|---|---|---|---|---|---|---|---|---|---|---|
| 29Mar86 10Hia9 | De Jeau | | 4 115 | 8 | 1 | 2hd | 3 1½ | 2½ | 1¾ | Hernandez C | 28.10 |
| 29Mar86 10Hia2 | Centenarian | | 5 115 | 5 | 6 | 3hd | 2½ | 1 1 | 2 1½ | Cruguet J | 3.40 |
| 20Mar86 9Hia1 | Ward Off Trouble | | 6 117 | 7 | 9 | 8½ | 10 2 | 8 4 | 3 1 | Suckie M C5 | 5.20 |
| 5Apr86 8Hia1 | Medieval Fashion | b | 6 115 | 4 | 7 | 5hd | 5hd | 4½ | 4hd | Gonzalez M A† | 7.50 |
| 15Mar86 11Hia8 | Ban the Blues | b | 7 119 | 6 | 11 | 9hd | 7hd | 5hd | 5½ | Hussey C | 14.50 |
| 22Mar86 10Hia2 | My Mac | b | 6 115 | 9 | 3 | 6 2 | 6 3 | 7hd | 6no | Pennisi F A | 7.20 |
| 20Mar86 9Hia7 | Opening Lead | b | 6 117 | 10 | 10 | 10½ | 9 1 | 6hd | 7½ | Pezua J M | 8.80 |
| 5Apr86 11Hia3 | Pitador | | 4 122 | 2 | 4 | 1 1 | 1hd | 3 2½ | 8 4 | Castaneda K | 3.30 |
| 11Apr86 9Hia9 | Lobbit | b | 4 110 | 3 | 8 | 7 1 | 8hd | 10 1½ | 9 1 | Lester R N5 | 26.00 |
| 9Nov85 9Crc10 | Crazy Moon | b | 6 117 | 11 | 2 | 11 | 11 | 11 | 10hd | Velez J A Jr | 56.80 |
| 29Mar86 10Hia1 | North Prospect | | 6 117 | 1 | 5 | 4 2½ | 4 1 | 9 2 | 11 | Centeno V R | 8.10 |

**OFF AT 4:57 Start good, Won driving. Time, :23⅕, :46, 1:10, 1:22⅗ Track fast.**

| $2 Mutuel Prices: | | | | |
|---|---|---|---|---|
| | 8-DE JEAU | 58.20 | 17.60 | 12.80 |
| | 5-CENTENARIAN | | 4.00 | 4.20 |
| | 7-WARD OFF TROUBLE | | | 4.40 |

**$2 PERFECTA 8-5 PAID $1168.20. $2 TRIFECTA 8-5-7 PAID $3461.60.**



There was more. Look at "Sassy Tudor" in the 6th race on April 16th.

**6 HIALEAH** 7 FURLONGS HIALEAH

**7 FURLONGS. (1.20⅗) MAIDEN CLAIMING. Purse $9,500 (Plus $1,500 FOA). 3- and 4-year-olds. Weights, 3-year-olds, 112 lbs. 4-year-olds, 122 lbs. Claiming Price $50,000; for each $2,500 to $45,000, 2 lbs.**

**Sassy Tudor** ● 2L2 — Ch. c. 3, by Sasafras—Princess Tudor, by King of the Tudors — $45,000 — Br.—Condon & Stoll Moses (Ky) — Tr.—Sanders Gregory E — Own.—Frisbie G H — 108 — Lifetime 6 0 0 0 $1,215 — 1986 5 M 0 0 $1,115 — 1985 1 M 0 0 $100

| | | | | | | | | | | | | | | | | | | | |
|---|---|---|---|---|---|---|---|---|---|---|---|---|---|---|---|---|---|---|---|
| 2Apr86- 7Hia | fst | 6f | :22⅖ | :45⅗ | 1:11 | 3↑Md 45000 | 8 | 7 | 7 5½ | 9 4½ | 9 14 | 8 9½ | Centeno V R | 113 | 99.80 | 75-21 | Mssr. Moment Away 123nk Shula113 1¼ TonightMyLove108 1 | Outrun | 12 |
| 15Feb86- 5GP | fst | 1⅛ | :48⅘ | 1:13⅘ | 1:46⅘ | Md Sp Wt | 8 | 9 | 9 18 | 10 37 | 10 47 | 10 51¼ | Hernandez C | 122 | 98.00 | — — | Clever Alibi 122 6 First Double 122 5½ Daytime Friend122 1½ | Outrun | 11 |
| 1Feb86- 5GP | fst | 6f | :22⅗ | :46 | 1:12 | Md Sp Wt | 5 | 8 | 5 1½ | 5 3½ | 9 18 | 9 16½ | Hernandez C | 122 | 26.00 | 63-27 | Lover's Cross 122 1 Dub Nhoc 122½ Charging Forbes 122 1½ | Outrun | 12 |
| 13Jan86- 4GP | fst | 6f | :22⅗ | :46⅗ | 1:12⅘ | Md Sp Wt | 1 | 6 | 4 1½ | 5 3½ | 4 8 | 4 12 | Hernandez C | 122 | 30.20 | 66-25 | Sweetheart So Long 122 2 Zango 122 8 Classic Move 122 2 | Outrun | 11 |
| 4Jan86- 3Crc | fst | 7f | :22⅘ | :46⅘ | 1:25⅘ | Md Sp Wt | 1 | 5 | 2hd | 2hd | 7 9 | 7 13½ | Hernandez C | 120 | 18.00 | 74-13 | J. O.Cross115 1½ GentleJourney120¾ CampaignRibbons120½ | Used up | 9 |
| 25Dec85- 1Crc | sly | 6f | :23⅘ | :47 | 1:12⅘ | Md Sp Wt | 2 | 3 | 1½ | 2½ | 4 4½ | 5 14½ | Hernandez C | 120 | 19.20 | 75-15 | Jig's Haven 120 9 Exuberback115 2 CampaignRibbons120 2½ | Steadied | 8 |

LATEST WORKOUTS Apr 10 Crc 4f fst :50⅘ b Mar 28 GP 5f fst 1:05 b Mar 7 GP 4f fst :50⅘ b

It's too soon to have forgotten Gregory Sanders and that $58.20 from a "2L7". Here we have another "2L" and now was not the time to be shy.

**SIXTH RACE** **Hialeah Park** **APRIL 16**

**7 FURLONGS. (1.20⅘) MAIDEN CLAIMING. Purse $9,500 (Plus $1,500 FOA). 3- and 4-year-olds. Weights, 3-year-olds, 112 lbs. 4-year-olds, 122 lbs. Claiming Price $50,000; for each $2,500 to $45,000, 2 lbs.**

**Value of race $9,500; value to winner $5,700; second $1,805; third $1,235; fourth $475; balance of starters $95 each. Mutuel pool $34,766. Perfecta Pool $30,406. Trifecta Pool $33,989.**

| Last Raced | Horse | Eqt.A.Wt | PP | St | ¼ | ½ | Str | Fin | Jockey | Cl'g Pr | Odds $1 |
|---|---|---|---|---|---|---|---|---|---|---|---|
| 2Apr86 $^7$Hia$^8$ | Sassy Tudor | 3 108 | 7 | 2 | $4^1$ | $4^{\frac{1}{2}}$ | $2^{2\frac{1}{2}}$ | $1^1$ | Gonzalez M A | 45000 | 22.90 |
| 31Mar86 $^{10}$Hia$^4$ | Enchanted Rebeau | b 3 112 | 1 | 5 | 7 | $6^{hd}$ | $4^4$ | $2^2$ | Velez J A Jr† | 50000 | 5.70 |
| 2Apr86 $^7$Hia$^3$ | Tonight My Love | b 3 107 | 6 | 1 | $1^4$ | $1^{1\frac{1}{2}}$ | $1^{\frac{1}{2}}$ | $3^2$ | Lester R N$^5$ | 50000 | .60 |
| 25Mar86 $^{10}$Hia$^6$ | Rigoberto | 4 118 | 3 | 3 | $5^{1\frac{1}{2}}$ | $5^{2\frac{1}{2}}$ | $3^{hd}$ | $4^4$ | Meade D Jr | 45000 | 13.90 |
| 8Apr86 $^6$Hia$^4$ | Gallant Idol | 3 108 | 4 | 7 | $6^{hd}$ | 7 | $6^{\frac{1}{2}}$ | $5^{\frac{3}{4}}$ | Cruguet J | 45000 | 4.40 |
| 22Mar86 $^6$Hia$^{10}$ | Buckchancer | 3 112 | 2 | 6 | $2^{hd}$ | $2^{hd}$ | $5^2$ | $6^1$ | Santiago J A | 50000 | 17.20 |
| 12Mar86 $^{10}$Hia$^5$ | Ice Laddie | 3 105 | 5 | 4 | $3^{1\frac{1}{2}}$ | $3^4$ | 7 | 7 | Carr J R$^7$ | 50000 | 7.10 |

**OFF AT 3:30. Start good, Won driving. Time, :23⅕, :46⅘, 1:12⅘, 1:26 Track fast.**

| $2 Mutuel Prices: | | | |
|---|---|---|---|
| 9-SASSY TUDOR | 47.80 | 16.20 | 3.60 |
| 1-ENCHANTED REBEAU | | 7.00 | 2.80 |
| 8-TONIGHT MY LOVE | | | 2.40 |

**$2 PERFECTA 9-1 PAID $238.20. $2 TRIFECTA 9-1-8 PAID $490.80.**

**Ch. c, by Sassafras—Princess Tudor, by King of the Tudors. Trainer Sanders Gregory E. Bred by Condon & Stoll Mmes (Ky).**

SASSY TUDOR in hand early, advanced steadily along the outside in the drive, gained command inside the final eighth, opened a clear lead, then lasted over ENCHANTED REBEAU. The latter outrun for a half, was coming on well at the finish. TONIGHT MY LOVE quickly sprinted clear, but gave way to the winner inside the final eighth. RIGOBERTO rallied approaching the head of the stretch to loom a threat to midstretch, but could not sustain the bid. GALLANT IDOL was outrun. BUCKCHANCER pressed the pace for a half, then weakened. ICE LADDIE was outrun.



The events of these two days were not my normal history. I *never* lead off with a winner; never get off to a decent start. Usually, it's the tail end. I would not have been put off by ten straight losers because I've learned to expect it.

At this point, I thought I'd died and gone to handicapper's heaven.

# CHAPTER SEVEN
# Further Analysis

# Further Analysis

Pleased with the results of my work, much of that year was spent at Calder Race Course, where I soon realized the need for a way to answer questions that came up between races. These questions involved trainers not yet familiar to me, and the information I generally needed was a "yes" or "no" to whether their entries represented a potential threat to something already in the works. My individual record file was too bulky to carry, so I settled on a book of graph pages; one page for each trainer in my files. This would be a book that could be carried easily and give me a statistical view of each trainer's history.

Next is an example of this graph sheet listing every Index that I was tracking. Each number in a box represents the finish position of one Index Runner, all trained by Jose A. Mendez.

**Mendez, Jose A.**

| Category | Values |
|---|---|
| FTS | 11 7 9 |
| 2TS | 3 |
| FTS2 | 5 9 8 6 10 6 10 4 7 11 5 6 7 9 2 10 7 6 8 11 8 6 |
| 2TS2 | 3 3 2 2 9 |
| L1-3 | 4 0 11 5 7 0 10 8 3 4 2 5 6 2 6 8 9 7 8 11 9 7 3 4 10 |
| L4-8 | 0 4 5 |
| L9up | |
| 2L1-3 | 2 1 |
| 2L4-8 | |
| 2L9up | |
| S | 7 9 12 8 9 7 |
| 2S | 11 |
| FTI | 5 |
| 2TT | 1 |
| Tt7 | 7 |
| Rt7 | 11 2 |
| StR | |
| FBK | 2 4 |

I used colored pens to show additional detail (that can not be seen in this black-and-white reproduction). A number written in red indicated the race was less than 7 furlongs. A yellow background for a red number identified a race of exactly 7 furlongs. Blue numbers indicated races around two turns and green told me the race was on the turf. A number with a circle around it was either a Stakes or Handicap race.

It was possible to get a pretty good picture of a trainer's probabilities with just a fast glance at this page.

From the prior example, one does not need colors to learn Jose Mendez is no threat with a 2-year-old first-time-starter or with any horse coming back from a short layoff. If I plan to wheel an exotic bet, I can save $2 on Jose, and chances are I will save several more dollars glancing at other trainer's showing similar histories. It all adds up.

The next example indicates exactly the opposite.

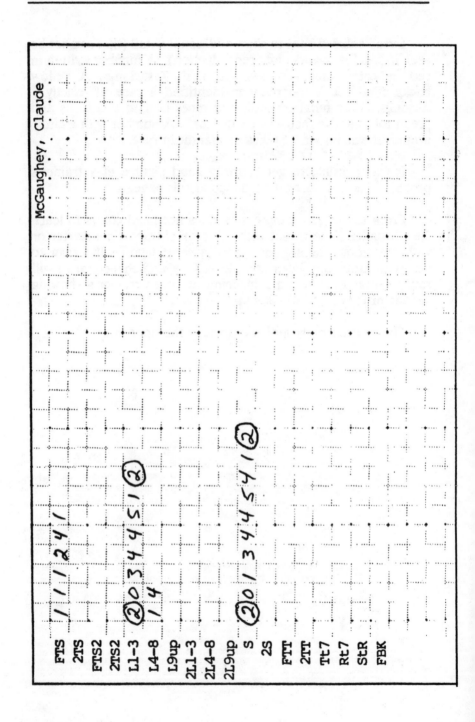

Claude McGaughey is very serious with his FTS; not only trying but winning! I should "key" him on top. This book proved very useful.

Bringing this statistical record up to date from the individual trainer's record of details, I came across a trainer whose graph sheet made my hand tremble. Jim Levitch normally runs in the midwest, shipping to Florida in the winter. His success with shippers was phenomenal, particularly the ones that had been rested a month or so before arriving in Florida. The small "s" next to a number indicates this horse was a shipper also. The statistical graph sheet illustrated the opportunity.

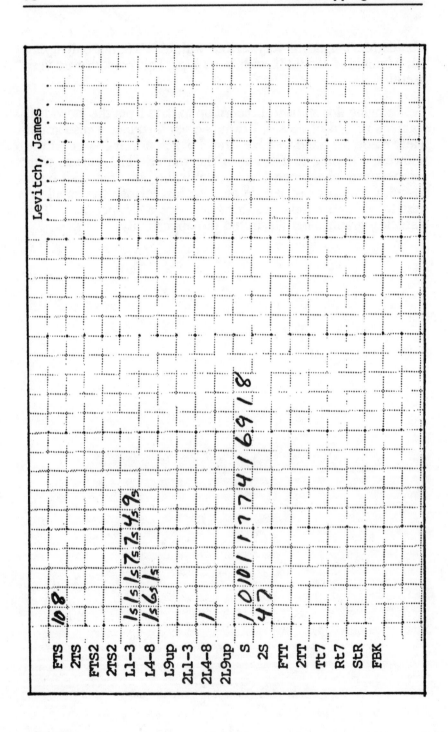

Looking at all those "1's" for his Layoff/Shippers sent me diving back into his individual record to learn if these runners were viable bets as determined by their odds. The three runners under "L1-3" paid 42-1, 9-1, and 10-1. The two winners under "L4-8" paid 3 1/2-1 and 5-1. The lone "2L4-8" paid 6 to 1. It was June before I got around to making this graph sheet. Talk about locking the barn!

By the time I discovered him, Jim Levitch had done his thing in Florida and gone. There was nothing to do but wait for him to return next winter. I now had a pretty good picture of what to expect from him and every one of his Shippers was going to get an automatic bet, blindfolded. I need to jump ahead in my story to round this out.

November came and my mouth began to water. If he didn't arrive by Christmas, I planned to send a cab for him. This proved unnecessary, and I remember cheering the first time I saw his name attached to a Calder entry on December 9th. Sure, Pruner's Gal ran 3rd, but I had a lot of confidence in Master Levitch.

His second Shipper, "Silver Witch" got home 1st; paying a paltry $7.20. His third Shipper, "Real Smart Girl," paid for all the aches and labor of the entire project: $111.40.

The question occurs to me - How often, using conventional techniques, is a winner selected that pays over 50 to 1?

With details in our records, evaluating a trainer is not a complicated process, and care must be taken to keep it simple. This was brought out in the previous chapter. When on the trail of something good there's a tendency to overdo, particularly when we're tempted to see what we *want* to see.

The information we seek, winning patterns, is not available to anybody reading a *Racing Form*. It is completely buried. We have set up a different kind of information source, tailored to enhance other aspects of racing facts. One of the first things we notice is how few trainers can accumulate a respectable number of "1's" and "2's" in the finish column.

### High Visibility Item

For most horseplayers, a First Time Starter is an enigma, obscurely bred, showing no merit other than a Handy workout. Back in the '70's, I can't remember betting one, but often I felt the excitement of their exotic payoffs. I was destroyed when one beat me out, thinking First Time Starters should not be allowed to win races. Make them run schooling races, like greyhounds. *Handicapping Trainers* has made the First Time Starter a very profitable animal. Their high visibility in the *Racing Form* means the gold is buried deeper than stats can see. If you don't have details, you don't have a shovel.

During the 1985-86 winter and spring meets at Gulfstream and Hialeah, Jorge Romero had baffled several hundred thousand bettors with horses that had never raced. He further confounded these unfortunates by showing few or no workouts relevant to today's race; and sent these neophytes out 7 furlongs or around two turns without the slightest hesitation. My first evaluation of Mr. Romero, in early April:

"ROMERO, Jorge Very successful with FTS and LAYOFFS showing few or no workouts. Will try and win at long odds. Uses quality horses. His 2TS or 3TS will get in the money at very long odds."

The entries on his record showed three wins and five seconds at prices most of us only dream about. Throw out the 78-1 and the 79-1 and he still averages better than 13-to-1 with the rest.

TRAINER; Romero, Jorge

PAGE 1

| RACE DATE | RACE # | TRACK | DIST | INDEX #1 | INDEX #2 | HORSE NAME | AGE | CLASS | LAST RACE Date, Track, Finish, Odds | WORKOUTS Since Last Race w/Interval | 1&2 ODDS | FIN | JOCKEY |
|---|---|---|---|---|---|---|---|---|---|---|---|---|---|
| 11/28/85 | 1 | CRC | 6 | FTS2 | | PERUGIA | 2 | X35 | | | 24.00 | 8 | Centeno |
| 12/06/85 | 1 | CRC | 6 | 2TS2 | | PERUGIA | 2 | X35 | 11/28/85CRC8924.00 | | 79.00 | 2 | Centeno |
| 12/19/85 | | CRC | 6 | FTS2 | | LAZARA | 2 | X50 | | | 19.00 | 7 | Pezua |
| 01/04/86 | 7 | CRC | 6 | L1.5 | | WOLTAN | 4 | NW3 | 11/28/85CRC8318.00 | | 3.50 | 5 | Centeno |
| 01/06/86 | 8 | CRC | 9 | L1 | | VALKYRIE | 3 | NW1 | 12/06/85CRC9318.00 | | 26.00 | 2 | Centeno |
| 01/16/86 | | GP | 6 | FTS | | RANCHWOOD | 4 | MSW | | | 92.00 | 6 | Pezua |
| 01/20/86 | 2 | GP | 6 | 2TS | | LAZARA | 3 | MSW | 12/19/85CRC7919.00 | | 26.00 | 8 | Pezua |
| 01/31/86 | 1 | GP | 7 | FTS | | FACT | 4 | MSW | | 14-3B6,23-6B6,1B,4B | 9.00 | 1 | Pezua |
| 01/31/86 | 4 | GP | 7 | FTS | | INDIO LOBO | 4 | MSW | | 14-3B6,22-6B,1B,5B | 8.00 | 2 | Centeno |
| 02/15/86 | 5 | GP | 8.5 | StR | | CLEVER ALIBI | 3 | MSW | | -5N;-,; | 3.00 | 1 | Romero |
| 02/15/86 | 3 | GP | 6 | 3TS | | LAZARA | 3 | MSW | 01/29/86GP3326.00 | | 78.00 | 2 | Pezua |
| 02/21/86 | 3 | GP | 8.5 | FTS | | VEGETARIANO | 4 | MSW | | -3B;-4B6;3B, | 12.60 | 2 | Pezua |
| 03/06/86 | 3 | GP | 7 | L2 | | RANCH WOOD | 4 | NW3 | 01/16/86GP6492.00 | | 5.00 | 6 | Pezua |
| 03/07/86 | 7 | GP | 6 | L2 | | WOLTAN | 3 | NW3 | 01/04/86CRC534.00 | -3B6;-,; | 24.00 | 1 | Centeno |
| 03/28/86 | 4 | HIA | 6 | FTS | | LUNA DE CANCUN | 3 | X22 | | | 25.00 | 6 | Centeno |
| 04/08/86 | 4 | HIA | 6 | 2TS | | LUNA DE CANCUN | 3 | X25 | 03/28/86HIA6925.00 | | 4.90 | 3 | Rodrigue |

This trainer looked so promising, I didn't wait 3 months before my next evaluation. In the middle of May I wrote:

"ROMERO, Jorge -- Few better with FTS but only under particular conditions. His greatest (not the only) success is with 4 year-old FTS going 7 furlongs or more. With 3 he has a win and 2 seconds at very good prices."

By the end of July, Romero had eight out of eight in the Exacta. Five of them should have been caught.

During that same period, J. Bert Sonnier ran twelve first time starters with which he had one place and one show. It would seem Mr. Sonnier was of a different mind than Mr. Romero when it came to FTS. When you have this kind of line on all the trainers at your track, winnowing a field of First Time Starters can be exciting.

Frank Gomez has a great reputation as a trainer but backing his FTS under any conditions will wipe you out. "Stealer" was his only FTS winner in 1986 out of 27 starters. Coincidentally, with his only FTS winner, he beat "Alonely Ballerina", also an FTS, trained by Stanley Hough, whose record shows a classic style with First Time Starters. He wins just often enough to keep the prices good. I had "Alonely Ballerina" that day, and recall seeing them around the far turn, coming into the stretch, "Alonely Ballerina" in front with "Stealer" second by a couple of lengths. I headed for the cashier. Why not? "Stealer" won't catch her. Gomez doesn't win with First Time Starters. Hough does. Simple.

Lesson #2001: You can beat the races, but you can't beat a race.

Looking back at the records of Frank Alexander and Jorge Romero, notice how the promise of good things practically jumps from the page. When indications of success are spotted in a trainer's record, a lot of wins with Index Runners, it doesn't take long to get to the gravy, if it's there. Many wins don't always turn up a pattern, but if one is there, it's hard to miss.

Often, a pattern of roses is well concealed by weeds.

**Negative Information**

Negative data in a trainer's file works in a large way to keep us from making a bad bet, allowing us to separate situations that are within the pattern, but carry a negative condition that identifies with failure. Another benefit; a great deal of negative information will discourage handicappers using statistics that say trainer K won only 4 of 20 with FTS. Average mutual $12. Not many can get too excited about betting $40 to win $8 when the money is tied up over the span of 20 races.

With the details being described here, we can learn that three of the four winners had something in common that could keep us from making ten or more of those losing bets. Betting $20 to get back $36 or $48 can be a bit more stimulating when you're working as the silent partner of a trainer with a pattern.

To better understand, we can look at the two situations with the highest visibility in the *Racing Form*, Claimed Horses and First Time Starters. When a trainer begins to click with either of these Index, the public won't be far behind. Conversely, when a trainer fails consistently, that, too, is soon evident.

It doesn't matter whether the trainer can not win or will not try. For practical purposes, the fact that trainer X is no threat with a Claimed Horse or a First Time Starter is a valuable bit of information; particularly if one is putting together an exotic ticket. There is only one way to learn, by tracking every incidence.

Most trainer's records will show spotty, undefinable performance through any level of research. Picking them apart in every conceivable way will produce nothing you can put a finger on. No degree of competence can be assigned here. Most, not all.

The trainer we are looking for, the one who is competent in this particular Index, succeeds because he knows his competition; he knows who the stumblers are when he enters his horse. This man's record will show *some* winners, but not necessarily enough to make them jump off the page. He can show an average of only 1 out of 15, paying 20 to 1 and turn out to be a gold mine.

Negative information isolates conditions a trainer has no liking for. It could be the distance, the surface, the time of year, the interval since his last race, the track, or an owner exerting too much influence. If you record all these facts as part of every incidence, you can zero in on the four or five of the above 15 when he'll be going for the money. For the statisticians he wins 1 out of 15. For us he wins 1 out of 5.

Where claimed horses are concerned, there are few trainers who can illustrate this point better that Peter Ferriola. His experience is very much like Neal Winick's, described earlier.

Examine Peter Ferriola's 1986 and 1987 record with claimed horses to see if there is profit in betting the first race after the claim. His record is poor in 1986 in every aspect, but in December things begin to pick up.

Ferricola, Peter     RECORD WITH CLAIMED HORSES FOR NEXT 3 RACES     PAGE 1

| CLAIM DATE | HORSE NAME | CLAIM RACE | CLAIM TRACK | CLAIM PRICE | FIN | NEW OWNER | INTERVAL #1 | CLASS OF 1st RACE | FIN #1 | ODDS | FIN #2 | ODDS | FIN #3 | ODDS |
|---|---|---|---|---|---|---|---|---|---|---|---|---|---|---|
| 12/04/86 | Glady H. | 7 | CRC | 40,000 | 5 | Nagle | 38 | ALW | 3 3 | 13 | 7 2 | 16 | 4 2 | 11 |
| 12/04/86 | Torrid Moment | 3 | CRC | 14,000 | 2 | Nagle | 20 | 18,000 | 3 2 | 6 | 7 2 | 13 | 0 | 0 |
| 12/06/86 | Father Roland | 9 | AQU | 25,000 | 8 | Riccio | 13 | 45,000 | 11 2 | 2 | 6 2 | 16 | 5 2 | 17 |
| 12/10/86 | Danning Glory | 3 | CRC | 17,000 | 1 | Nagle | 50 | 25,000 | 3 2 | 28 | 1 2 | 3 | 6 2 | 4 |
| 12/10/86 | Hoist N' Hail | 4 | CRC | 20,000 | 4 | Nagle | 35 | MSW | 4 2 | 2 | 7 2 | 8 | 2 2 | |
| 12/14/86 | West Maui | 7 | CRC | 45,000 | 3 | Vee Pee Jay Stab | 15 | ALW | 4 2 | 2 | 3 2 | 6 | 2 2 | |
| 12/16/86 | Draconic Mark | 6 | CRC | 8,500 | 1 | Nagle | 7 | 16,000 | 7 2 | 11 | 3 2 | 6 | 2 2 | |
| 12/16/86 | Sea Escape | 8 | CRC | 25,000 | 2 | Nagle | 10 | 35,000 | 7 2 | 24 | 7 2 | 15 | 9 2 | 16 |
| 12/17/86 | Sultry Flower | 6 | CRC | MD CL | 2 | Gold-N-Oats Stab | 33 | MD CL | 12 2 | 5 | 8 2 | 32 | 10 2 | 16 |
| 12/18/86 | Diamond Joy | 10 | CRC | MD CL | | Nagle | 3 | MD CL | 1 2 | 4 | | | | |
| 12/18/86 | Mr. J. V. | 3 | CRC | 12,500 | 1 | Nagle | 8 | 18,000 | 2 2 | 14 | 3 2 | 22 | 1 2 | 7 |
| 12/18/86 | Shy Gold | 3 | CRC | 30,000 | 1 | Nagle | 6 | 50,000 | 6 2 | 8 | 7 2 | 14 | 1 2 | 7 |
| 12/19/86 | Saintly Chief | 1 | CRC | MD CL | 2 | Nagle | 20 | MSW | 2 2 | 3 | 1 2 | 1 | | |
| 12/19/86 | Thimbleful Of Joy | 4 | CRC | MD CL | | Nagle | 96 | MD CL | 1 2 | 5 | | | | |
| 12/20/86 | Majestic Empire | 8 | 2 | 35,000 | 7 | Riccio | 15 | 70,000 | 2 2 | 30 | 1 2 | 5 | 10 2 | 10 |
| 12/21/86 | Captain Albert | 8 | CRC | 40,000 | 2 | Nagle | 22 | 50,000 | 3 2 | 4 | | | | |
| 12/21/86 | Sir Hasten | 10 | CRC | 16,000 | 2 | Nagle | 13 | 15,000 | 2 2 | 4 | 9 2 | 6 | 10 2 | 10 |
| 01/06/87 | Whoop De Doo | 4 | CRC | 20,000 | 1 | Nagle | 23 | 25,000 | 3 2 | 3 | | | | |
| 01/15/87 | Dale's Folly | 4 | AQU | 25,000 | 4 | Nagle | 6 | 45,000 | 3 2 | 43 | 1 2 | 5 | | |
| 01/16/87 | Nurse Anesthetist | 2 | HIA | 12,500 | 3 | Nagle | 8 | 16,000 | 2 2 | 5 | 3 2 | 21 | | |
| 01/16/87 | Shesa Snap | 3 | HIA | 6,500 | 5 | Nagle | 31 | 10,500 | 10 2 | 24 | | | | |
| 01/18/87 | Ian Charles Pet | 3 | HIA | 25,000 | 1 | Nagle | 19 | 40,000 | 9 2 | 4 | 1 2 | 5 | | |
| 01/19/87 | French Express | 9 | AQU | 20,000 | 1 | Nagle | 9 | 27,000 | 9 2 | 8 | 1 2 | 8 | | |
| 02/06/87 | Macbest | 3 | HIA | 40,000 | 1 | Baselice | 22 | HCP | 5 2 | 14 | | | | |
| 02/06/87 | Scott's Jet | 1 | HIA | 35,000 | 5 | Nagle | 35 | ALW | 4 2 | 35 | 7 2 | 6 | 4 2 | 6 |
| 02/06/87 | Sparkes Around | 1 | AQU | 25,000 | 9 | Nagle | 22 | 32,500 | 5 2 | 17 | 6 2 | 8 | 7 2 | 2 |
| 02/14/87 | Aquahero | 7 | AQU | 17,500 | 2 | Vee Pee Jay Stab | 4 | 22,500 | 12 2 | 5 | 11 2 | 9 | 6 2 | 1 |
| 02/14/87 | Skies Over Vienna | 11 | HIA | 35,000 | 10 | Gold-N-Oats Stab | 89 | MSW | 3 2 | 8 | 2 2 | 6 | | |
| 02/15/87 | Dewar's Hall | 2 | HIA | 6,250 | 11 | Walker | 8 | 8,000 | 7 2 | 46 | | | | |
| 03/09/87 | Brasov | 4 | AQU | 17,500 | 7 | Gold-N-Oats Stab | 31 | 17,500 | 9 2 | 10 | 4 2 | 7 | 5 2 | 7 |

Ferricja, Peter          RECORD WITH CLAIMED HORSES FOR NEXT 3 RACES

| CLAIM DATE | HORSE NAME | CLAIM RACE | CLAIM TRACK | CLAIM PRICE | FIN | NEW OWNER | INTERVAL #1 | CLASS OF 1st RACE | FIN #1 | ODDS | FIN #2 | ODDS | FIN #3 | ODDS |
|---|---|---|---|---|---|---|---|---|---|---|---|---|---|---|
| 04/01/87 | One Bon Bon | 4 | AQU | 50,000 | 3 | Ricco | 10 | ALW | ① a | 1 | a | | a | |
| 04/13/87 | Full Stocking | 1 | AQU | 17,500 | 3 | Basilic | 19 | 22,500 | 10 a | 7 | 11 a | 26 | a | |
| 04/15/87 | Raise A Beat | 3 | AQU | 32,500 | 1 | Riccio | 9 | ALW | ③ a | 1 | 1 a | 2 | a | |
| 04/20/87 | Flying Hope | 1 | AQU | 17,500 | 3 | Muro | 7 | 25,000 | 3 a | 6 | 2 a | 4 | 1 a | 1 |
| 04/29/87 | Match Speed | 3 | AQU | 17,500 | 3 | Gold-N-Oats Stab | 12 | 30,000 | 4 a | 9 | 4 a | 3 | 6 a | 9 |
| 05/09/87 | Twenty Degree Bank | 1 | BEL | 17,500 | 2 | Gold-N-Oats Stab | 21 | 22,500 | 2 a | 1 | 3 a | 2 | a | |
| 05/16/87 | What Intensity | 3 | GP | 35,000 | 3 | Gold-N-Oaks Stab | 19 | 45,000 | 2 a | 5 | 2 a | 5 | 1 a | 3 |
| 05/24/87 | Tarnished Gold | 4 | BEL | 45,000 | 5 | Gold-N-Oaks Stab | 35 | ALW | 6 a | 4 | 4 a | 6 | 1 a | 1 |
| 06/08/87 | Drone On And On | 2 | BEL | M035,000 | 4 | Bara Stable | 35 | M035,000 | 1 a | 4 | a | | a | |
| 06/14/87 | Truth Be Told | 1 | BEL | 17,500 | 2 | Ricco | 11 | 25,000 | ① a | 3 | 3 a | 26 | 10 a | 18 |
| 06/15/87 | Personal Problem | 2 | BEL | 45,000 | 9 | Nagle | 16 | 45,000 | 11 a | 5 | 3 a | 7 | a | |
| 06/17/87 | Ricts Delivery | 2 | BEL | 45,000 | 2 | Vee Pee Jay Stab | 12 | ALW | 3 a | 7 | 2 a | 3 | a | |
| 06/22/87 | Fire Haze | 5 | BEL | 25,000 | 5 | Nagle | 32 | 25,000 | 4 a | 2 | 7 a | 27 | 5 a | 10 |
| 06/26/87 | Ebony Rig | 1 | BEL | 30,000 | 4 | Nagle | 9 | 45,000 | 3 a | 15 | a | | a | |
| 07/13/87 | Fugie | 2 | BEL | 35,000 | 7 | Riccio | 13 | ALW | ① 6 | | a | | a | |
| 07/20/87 | Kevelrout | 3 | BEL | 35,000 | 5 | Nagle | 9 | 45,000 | 6 a | 9 | 3 a | 2 | 1 a | 1 |

Ferriola, Peter        RECORD WITH CLAIMED HORSES FOR NEXT 3 RACES        PAGE 2

| CLAIM DATE | HORSE NAME | CLAIM RACE | CLAIM TRACK | CLAIM PRICE | FIN | NEW OWNER | INTERVAL #1 | CLASS OF 1st RACE | FIN | #1 ODDS | FIN | #2 ODDS | FIN | #3 ODDS |
|---|---|---|---|---|---|---|---|---|---|---|---|---|---|---|
| 07/22/87 | Time For Emeralds | 2 | BEL | 35,000 | 2 | Nagle | 10 | ALW | 2 | 2 5 | 2 | 2 5 | 2 | 2 2 |
| 07/23/87 | Chyonofugi | 3 | BEL | 35,000 | 6 | Nagle | 6 | ALW | 6 | 2 40 | 1 | 2 4 | | 2 |
| 07/24/87 | Mixed Emotions | 5 | BEL | 25000 | 3 | Vee-Pee-Jay | 22 | 45000 | 5 | 2 9 | 5 | 2 4 | 1 | 2 5 |
| 07/30/87 | No Question | 1 | BEL | 20,000 | 3 | Kaulker | 15 | 20,000 | 4 | 2 7 | 2 | 2 6 | 2 | 2 5 |
| 08/17/87 | Star Brilliant | 7 | MTH | 35000 | 5 | Gold-N-Oats | 38 | 32500 | 4 | 2 3 | 1 | 2 1 | | 2 |
| 08/26/87 | Visible Force | 4 | MTH | 14000 | 4 | Gold-N-Oats | 60 | 15500 | 1 | 2 10 | | | | 2 |
| 09/03/87 | Sir Prize Birthday | 7 | MTH | 25,000 | 1 | Gold-N-Oats Stab | 18 | 32,500 | 5 | 2 2 | | | | 2 |
| 09/09/87 | Press My Buzzer | 2 | BEL | 50000 | 3 | Bara | 14 | ALW | 6 | (①) 2 5 | 5 | 2 20 | 5 | 2 1 |
| 10/05/87 | Truth Be Told | 1 | BEL | 35000 | 2 | Riccio | 91 | 17500 | 2 | 2 1 | | 2 6 | | 2 |
| 10/06/87 | Heisted | 5 | MED | 40000 | 1 | Gold N Oats Stab | 23 | ALW | 1 | 2 2 | 1 | 2 6 | | 2 |
| 10/18/87 | Nice Core | 9 | BEL | 25000 | 4 | Gold-N-Oats Stab | 32 | 30000 | 2 | 2 1 | | | | 2 |
| 10/18/87 | Golden Sweetheart | 1 | CRC | 60000 | 1 | Gold-N-Oats | 27 | 75000 | 2 | 2 1 | 7 | 2 1 | 2 | 2 1 |
| 10/31/87 | Jarreau | 2 | CRC | 20000 | 1 | Nagle, K. | 29 | 70000 | 4 | 2 3 | 5 | 2 4 | 4 | 2 2 |
| 11/01/87 | Links Of Gold | 6 | AQU | 50000 | 1 | Nagle, Kerry | 11 | ALW | 2 | 2 9 | 4 | 2 3 | 4 | 2 2 |
| 11/03/87 | Yosi's Lad | 1 | CRC | 15000 | 4 | Nagle, K | 23 | 30000 | 2 | 2 1 | 1 | 2 4 | 1 | 2 4 |
| 11/04/87 | Harry N' Bernie | 8 | CRC | 40,000 | 2 | Nagle K | 29 | 50,000 | 2 | 2 1 | 5 | 2 4 | 1 | 3 3 |
| 11/04/87 | Lulu Dancer | 5 | CRC | 25000 | 2 | Nagle, K. | 26 | 32500 | 5 | 2 1 | 8 | 2 4 | | 3 |
| 11/05/87 | Hollywood Barb | 5 | CRC | MD25000 | 1 | Nagle | 32 | 45000 | 1 | 2 2 | | | | 2 |
| 11/28/87 | Placid Waters | 3 | AQU | 32500 | 5 | Riccio | 9 | 45000 | (⑤) | (③) 3 | | | | 2 |
| 12/03/87 | Superb Time | 9 | AQU | 47500 | 4 | Gold N Oats Stab | 35 | 25000 | 1 | 2 1 | 1 | 2 1 | 2 | 2 1 |
| 12/12/87 | Silky Appeal | 1 | HIA | 17500 | 1 | Nagel | 376 | 25000 | 5 | 2 5 | 2 | 2 2 | 2 | 2 1 |
| 12/16/87 | Ballet Birdie | 7 | HIA | 19000 | 3 | Nagle | 4 | 45000 | 2 | 2 9 | 3 | 2 2 | 4 | 2 5 |
| 12/16/87 | Ring For Peace | 1 | HIA | 35000 | 1 | Nagle | 6 | 28000 | 8 | 2 9 | 7 | 2 5 | 2 | 2 5 |
| 12/20/87 | Daylight Saving | 3 | HIA | 16000 | 2 | Nagle | | 28000 | 8 | 2 9 | 2 | 2 6 | 2 | 2 6 |
| 12/31/87 | Go For Commodore | 4 | HIA | 20000 | 4 | Nagle | 29 | 50000 | 3 | 2 7 | 1 | 2 2 | | 2 |

His record for 1987 shows 54 runbacks after a claim (we are tracking only the first race after the Claim in this example). He won with ten. After betting $108, we broke about even. Statistically speaking, this is a waste of time. With additional details, we might learn that most of his wins were ridden by a certain jockey; or most were around two turns. There are as many areas to search as the number of details we track. In the above example, details will tell us that a very heavy profit exists if we know *who owns the horse.*

At $2 each, 24 runbacks for Kerry Nagle cost $48; we got back $6. For Gold-N-Oats we bet $26 and got back $32. For Baselice, Vee pee Jay, Walker, Muro, Bara and Kaulker we bet $20 and got back $10. When we get to his work for Riccio, big smiles. He ran back seven and won with five. (The two horses that lost the first race after the claim won the next time out). The question is, at what point did we discover this was a good thing and start backing it at the window? A good time would have been after his win with "One Bon Bon" on April 1. Examine the record and decide for yourself.

Turning back to Jorge Romero's record, we learned in very few races he will not only try, but will succeed with a First Time Starter. Examining his losers for common factors saved a large chunk of the profit from being eroded by animals he had no intention of pushing, in his case, 3-year-olds and entries going only 6 furlongs.

See Romero's record with FTS through July '86. My only complaint is, he did too well, too quickly. With such a high visibility Index, the public gobbled him up.

| | |
|---|---|
| Ranchwood | 6th @ 92-1 |
| Fact | 1st @ 9-1 |
| Indio Lobo | 2nd @ 8-1 |
| Vegeteriano | 2nd @ 12-1 |
| Luna de Cancun | 6th @ 25-1 |
| Grenagle II | 9th @ 5-1 |
| Woodcock | 1st @ 10-1(disqualified to 2nd) |

| | |
|---|---|
| Espacio | 5th @ 3-1 |
| Palera | 1st @ 2-1 |
| Pirandello | 3rd @ 11-1 |
| Ra | 2nd @ 2-1 |
| Found | 2nd @ 1-1 |
| Estano | 6th @ 5-1 |
| Play Ball | 8th @ 3-1 |
| Dr. Liddle | 2nd @ 14-1 |

"Woodcock" was my first bet on a Romero FTS. The negative conditions evident told me to pass "Espacio, Pirandello" and "Play Ball."

"Palera" won and "Ra, Found" and "Dr. Liddle" all ran 2nd. Only "Estano" qualified and was a loser.

Through the end of 1986, I tried to get through all the trainer's records in my file every three months. This way, I learned if earlier conclusions were holding up; also, the additional data brought out things in other trainers that previously showed too few samples for conclusions. At the end of July, Mr. Alexander's record offered considerably more than at the beginning. It is included here in the event that you want to know how your own analysis of his previous record held up.

TRAINER:   Alexander, Frank

| RACE DATE | RACE # | TRACK | DIST | INDEX #1 | INDEX #2 | HORSE NAME | AGE | CLASS | LAST RACE Date, Track, Finish, Odds | WORKOUTS Since Last Race w/Interval 1&2 | ODDS | FIN | JOCKEY |
|---|---|---|---|---|---|---|---|---|---|---|---|---|---|
| 11/30/85 | 3 | CRC | ? | FTS2 | | MAEGIE GAYLORD | 2 | MSW | | -5B6,-5B,, | 2.00 | 3 | Vasquez |
| 12/19/85 | 7 | CRC | 8.5 | S | | ANNIE BLUEEYES | 4 | C26 | 11/25/85AQU8Q13.60 | -4B,-,, | 51.00 | 1 | Lester |
| 12/27/85 | 10 | CRC | 6 | L7 | | NAHEMA | 3 | N22 | 05/11/85CRC207.00 | -4E5,-4B,, | 1.00 | 1 | Vasquez |
| 01/07/86 | 3 | CRC | 5? | L3 | I | DERBY LADY | 4 | NW2 | 10/21/85ENG11011.0 | -4B,-43,-5B,5B | 13.00 | 1 | Vasquez |
| 01/07/86 | 4 | CRC | 6 | FTS | | FANTASTIC ROBBER | 3 | MSW | | -5B,-5B6,6B6,5B | 14.00 | 1 | Vasquez |
| 01/05/86 | 8 | GP | BT | L3 | | WATCH WORD | 5 | NW3 | 10/19/85CRC403.50 | -4B,-5H,5H,4B | 10.00 | 1 | Vasquez |
| 01/17/86 | 6 | GP | 7 | FTS | | NAKEESHA | 3 | MSW | | -4B6,-5B6,5B,5B6 | 6.00 | 7 | McCauley |
| 01/27/86 | 4 | GP | 7 | FTS | | SWEET SHERYL | 3 | MSW | | -5B,-4B6,5B,5B | 8.00 | 3 | McCauley |
| 01/29/86 | 4 | GP | 7 | FTS | | ENTERTAIN | 3 | MSW | | -4B6,-4B6,5B,4B | 6.00 | 4 | Vasquez |
| 02/06/86 | 6 | GP | 7 | FTS | | ETERNAL VOW | 3 | MSW | 02/06/86GP408.00 | -5B,-5B6,4B6,4B | 5.00 | 6 | Lester |
| 02/17/86 | 6 | GP | 7 | 2TS | | ETERNAL VOW | 3 | MSW | 12/25/85CRC1026.00 | -3H6,-,, | 6.00 | 6 | Lester |
| 02/26/86 | 3 | GP | 8.5T | L2 | | STRAMAR | 4 | NW9 | | -4B,-5B,4H,5B | 12.00 | 12 | St. Leon |
| 03/01/86 | 3 | GP | 6 | FTS | | DOC CONNOR | 3 | MSW | | | 6.00 | 1 | St. Leon |
| 03/06/86 | 9 | GP | BT | L2 | | PURPLE COMET | 5 | NW5 | 01/21/86GP403.50 | -5H,-4H,6B,5H | 7.00 | 6 | Perret |
| 03/17/86 | 9 | HIA | 7 | L6 | S | CHOCOLATE SWISS | 3 | STK | 09/22/86HOO231.00 | -5B,-6B,5H6,4B | 6.00 | 6 | Bailey |
| 03/19/86 | 6 | HIA | 6 | L5 | S | NARROW ESCAPE | 3 | NW1 | 10/20/86BEL641.50 | -5B,-5B,5B,5B | 35.00 | 7 | Riveria |
| 03/29/86 | 8 | HIA | 8.5 | L2 | | DARBY LADY | 4 | NW3 | 01/21/86GP902.00 | -6B,-5B,5B,5B | 15.00 | 2 | Perret |
| 04/05/86 | 8 | HIA | 7 | L2 | | WATCH WORD | 5 | C45 | 02/10/86GP627.00 | -4B,34-4B6,5B, | 6.00 | 5 | Lester |
| 04/07/86 | 8 | HIA | 6 | L6 | | KID COLIN | 3 | NW3 | 02/28/86BEL626.00 | -4B,-3H,5H,3H6 | 5.00 | 1 | Perret |
| 04/10/86 | 8 | HIA | 8.5T | 2L5 | S | NARROW ESCAPE | 3 | X40 | 03/19/86HIA7205.00 | -4B6,-5B,4B6,5B | 3.00 | 1 | Perret |
| 04/12/86 | 4 | HIA | 6 | FTS | | COOL IT | 3 | MSW | | -4B6,-5B,4B6,5B | 8.00 | 8 | Squartin |

TRAINER: Alexander, Frank

| RACE DATE | RACE #TRACK DIST | INDEX #1 | INDEX #2 | HORSE NAME | AGE | CLASS | LAST RACE Date, Track Finish, Odds | WORKOUTS Since Last Race w/Interval 1&2 ODDS | FIN | JCKEY |
|---|---|---|---|---|---|---|---|---|---|---|
| 04/15/86 8 HIA 8.5T | L2 | | OK FINE | 4 | NW1 | 02/13/86BPB05.50 | 5-4B,12-5B,5H,4S | 9.80 | 1 | Soto |
| 04/23/86 7 HIA 7 | FTS | | BICKERSON | 3 | X40 | | -5B,-4BG,4BG,5B | 8.00 | 10 | Squartin |
| 04/27/86 11 HIA 9T | FTT | | BIEN SUR | 3 | MSW | 03/21/86YAM502.00 | -5B,-4B,, | 12.00 | 7 | Soto |
| 05/03/86 6 HIA 6 | FTS | | STOP DE LEA | 3 | MSW | | -5BG,-5B,4BG,4B | 6.00 | 4 | Lester |
| 05/04/86 1 HIA 9T | FTS | | PAUL MURPHY | 2 | X12 | | -3B,-5BG,5B,4BG | 4.00 | 7 | Aceveto |
| 05/11/86 5 HIA 9T | 2TT | | BIEN SUR | 3 | MSW | 04/27/86HIA7B12.00 | -4B,-,, | 3.00 | 2 | Lester |
| 05/12/86 8 HIA 7 | L2 | | MAGGIE GAYLORD | 3 | NW1 | 03/01/86BPS02.00 | -4B,-3H,5H,5B | 2.00 | 2 | St.Leon |
| 05/18/86 7 HIA 8.5T | L9 | S | BROADWAY HARRY | 6 | NW$ | 07/04/86GSP07.00 | 14-6B,-5B,5B,6B | 8.00 | 4 | Gonzalez |
| 05/18/86 2 HIA 7 | FTS | | JAMIE'S FAMILY | 3 | X12 | | -5B,25-5BG,5B,4BG | 7.00 | 1 | Lester |
| 05/30/86 8 CRC 6 | L7 | | BROOM BOSS | 4 | NW2 | 10/19/85CRC406.00 | 15-6B,-5B,4B,5B | 12.00 | 11 | St.Leon |
| 05/30/86 9 CRC 6 | L2 | | SHOW DANCER | 4 | HCP | 04/05/86HIA9B.00 | 12-5B,-5B,4B,4B | 6.00 | 7 | St.Leon |
| 05/31/86 8 CRC 8.5 | L2 | | PURPLE COMET | 5 | HCP | 04/11/86HIA7B1.50 | 15-4H,-5B,5H, | 4.00 | 1 | Smith |
| 06/01/86 6 CRC 7 | L8 | | AT THE LIMIT | 3 | C15 | 09/23/85CRC402.50 | -6B,-4BG,5B,5B | 8.00 | 8 | Misiewic |
| 06/01/86 9 CRC 7 | L2 | | KID COLIN | 3 | STK | 04/07/86HIA5B3.00 | 21-1H,-7B,5BG,4H | 7.00 | 1 | St.Leon |
| 06/04/86 6 CRC 6 | L1.5 | | BICKERSON | 5 | X25 | 04/23/86HIA16B28.0 | -5B,-4BG,5B,5B | 12.00 | 12 | Lester |
| 06/07/86 7 CRC 7 | L8 | | D.WHITE | 3 | NW$ | 10/07/85CRC302.00 | -4B,25-5B,5B,5BG | 3.00 | 5 | St.Leon |
| 06/08/86 6 CRC 7 | L4 | | ENTERTAIN | 3 | MSW | 01/29/86GP3014.00 | -4B,14-4B,4B,3B | 4.00 | 1 | Lester |
| 06/08/86 8 CRC 7 | L5 | | SANDY BOTTOM BOY | 3 | MSW | 12/25/85CRCR4.00 | -5B,14-5B,5B,5B | 5.00 | 5 | St.Leon |
| 06/11/86 10 CRC 10 | L2 | | COOL IT | 3 | X30 | 04/12/86HIA8B12.00 | -5B,-5B,4B,, | 12.00 | 4 | Lester |
| 06/12/86 9 CRC 6.5 | L9 | | INCA KING | 4 | NW2 | 07/13/85S31.AA | -5B,2B-4B,, | 65.00 | 1 | Lester |
| 06/13/86 9 CRC 6.5 | L5 | | LIFE'S LIGHT | 5 | NW1 | 12/31/85CRCR61.00 | -5B,-5B,5B,5B | 3.00 | 1 | St.Leon |
| 06/14/86 2 CRC 7 | FTS | | AMADIA | 3 | MSW | | | 5.00 | 8 | St.Leon |
| 06/22/86 4 CRC 6 | FTS | | RIVA LARK | 3 | X30 | | | 3.00 | 2 | Lester |
| 07/03/86 4 CRC 5.5 | FTS2 | | CAGE RATTLER | 2 | X30 | | | 16.00 | 12 | Lester |
| 07/05/86 2 CRC 5.5 | FTS2 | | SEAHAWK BLUE | 2 | X30 | | | 6.00 | 4 | Lester |
| 07/16/86 6 CRC 6 | FTS | | RHONDA'S RING | 3 | X20 | | | 6.00 | 4 | Squartin |
| 07/19/86 3 CRC 6 | FTS2 | | IFISH CHILI | 2 | MSW | 05/12/86ARB026.00 | -4B,-4BG,5BG,4B | 4.00 | 4 | St.Leon |
| 07/27/86 1 CRC 6 | L9 | S | BY CONSENSUS | 3 | X25 | 11/01/86CD506.00 | -5B,-5BG,5B,4B | 22.00 | 9 | Smith |
| 07/27/86 1 CRC 6 | L8 | S | SUM THUMPER | 3 | X25 | 01/13/86BPA04.00 | -4BG,2B-4B,4B,3B | 9.00 | 5 | St.Leon |
| 07/30/86 2 CRC 6 | L6 | | EXPANSIVE | 4 | C14 | 07/05/86CRC202.50 | -4BG,-5B,5B,4B | 4.00 | 3 | Lester |
| 07/30/86 7 CRC 8T | FTT | | KID COLIN | 3 | NW$ | 07/05/86CRC202.50 | -5B,-5B,, | 1.00 | 1 | St.Leon |
| 07/30/86 10 CRC 8T | L1.5 | | AMADIA | 3 | MSW | 06/14/86CRC863.00 | -4BG,-5B,4B,4BG | 4.00 | 7 | St.Leon |

TRAINER:   Alexander, Frank                                                          PAGE 2

| RACE DATE | RACE # | TRACK | DIST | INDEX #1 | INDEX #2 | HORSE NAME | AGE | CLASS | LAST RACE Date, Track, Finish, Odds | WORKOUTS Since Last Race w/Interval 1&2 | ODDS | FIN | JOCKEY |
|---|---|---|---|---|---|---|---|---|---|---|---|---|---|
| 08/03/86 | 3 | CRC | 6.5 | L3 | | STOP DE LEA | 3 | MSW | 05/03/86H1A427.00 | -6B,-5B,4B | 3.00 | 7 | Espinoza |
| 06/10/86 | 3 | CRC | 6 | FTS | | BEDDAY'S LADY | 3 | MSW | | | 10.00 | 1 | Gonzalez |
| 06/10/86 | 8 | CRC | 8T | FTT | | SHOW DANCER | 4 | NW6 | 07/12/86CRC8G13.00 | -5B,-6B,, | 6.00 | 1 | St. Lero |
| 09/10/86 | 9 | CRC | 9T | 2TT | | MAGGIE GAYLORD | 3 | STK | 07/11/86CRC222.90 | -5M,-5B,, | 12.00 | 5 | St. Leon |
| 05/13/86 | 2 | CRC | 6.5 | 2L9 | | BY CONSENSUS | 3 | | | | 3.00 | 1 | Espinoza |
| 05/16/86 | 5 | CRC | 8.5T | L1.5 | | D. WHITE | 5 | C50 | 07/06/86CRC393.00 | 15-5B,-5B,5H, | 2.00 | 4 | St. Leon |
| 06/17/86 | 1A | CRC | 8.5 | L1.5 | | SANDY BOTTOM BOY | 3 | C25 | 06/28/86CRC726.00 | -5B,-5B,5B,4B | 6.00 | 3 | St. Leon |
| 06/24/86 | 6 | CRC | 8.5 | 2TT | | INCA KING | 4 | NW2 | 09/03/86CRC8021.00 | -3B,-5M,, | 20.00 | 9 | Espinoza |
| 06/28/86 | 7 | CRC | 7 | Rt7 | | D. WHITE | 5 | C50 | 08/16/86CRC404.00 | | 3.00 | 3 | St. Leon |
| 09/31/86 | 7 | CRC | 8.5T | FTT | | ENTERTAIN | 3 | NW3 | 08/16/86CRC202.00 | -4H,-,, | 2.90 | 1 | St. Leon |
| 09/04/86 | 2 | CRC | 8.5 | L2 | | COOL IT | 3 | X12 | 06/27/86CRC9612.00 | -4B5,-5B,55,4B | 10.00 | 9 | Gonzalez |
| 09/06/86 | 5 | CRC | 8.5 | L1.5 | | BIEN SUR | 3 | MSW | 07/20/86CRC508.00 | -5B,-5B,5B,5B | 5.00 | 5 | Gonzalez |
| 09/10/86 | 3 | CRC | 7 | FTS | | THRILL HILL | 3 | MSW | | -4B5,-5B5,59.5BG | 6.00 | 6 | Gonzalez |
| 09/13/86 | 4 | CRC | 6 | FIS2 | | GREAT INVADER | 2 | MSW | | -4B,-5B5,5B,4½ | 6.61 | 1 | St. Leon |

"ALEXANDER, Frank  With 17 FTS and FTS2 he is 2-2-2 (WPS). His best performance is in the 1st start (dirt or turf) after a Layoff of 2 to 3 months. In this he is winning 6 of 12 at odds of 13, 10, 10, 7, 7 and 6 to 1..."

Back in April, when we first picked up his pattern, he had won three out of six times, at 13, 10 and 7 to 1. By the end of July he ran that pattern six more times, winning with *another three* (one was "OK Fine"). We must have caught another at 7 to 1 and a 6 to 1 from the other four races.

All we had to do to cash these tickets was look for, "Frank Alexander with a L2, L2.5, L3, L3.5". We didn't have to 'handicap' the race because he had already done that for us, when he *entered* his horse. He knew *where* to enter his horse. He *knew*! And what's more, he had already proven to us he knew what he was doing; a *proven* professional. Where can we find the nerve to second-guess him? He's made it *easy* for us. All we had to do was "spot the entry" and "be there with our money."

"... he was second with two others at 4-1 and 1-1; third with another at 11-1. (Eight of eleven in the exacta, nine of eleven in the triple). His performance is poor with Layoffs of 1.5 months and more than 4 months where he is three for sixteen; all at short odds. He will repeat. The tote board is not an indicator of his intentions."

Obviously, the tote is no indicator with the prices he's getting. His record is beginning to fill out and we near a point we can find common factors among his losers (within the Layoff Index). He does almost nothing at 6 furlongs. All his winners were at 7 furlongs or more. It appears he uses 6 furlongs for conditioning.

In my research, the positive aspects of trainer's patterns came slowly; requiring many samples of a particular situation that, in itself, had many sub conditions. Negative information shows up immediately, generally reinforced by subsequent samples. 95% of the research verifies negative information.

Entries of a trainer mentioned earlier, J. Bert Sonnier, generally command respect and a lot of betting activity, but with FTS, Layoffs or Shippers, forget him.

This is very important knowledge regardless of the kind of bet you plan to make. Knowing when favored entries will only be cruising gives you the edge on potentially large payoffs. The question, "Why did he try with this one and not with that one?" will often be answered by a close examination of negative information.

# CHAPTER EIGHT
# Going With the Pros

# Going With the Pros

At this point, the gold is scattered about my feet. I need only pick it up and see *what* belongs to *whom*.

Every Index that was being researched was listed and, placed next to each, the name of the trainer who, through a sufficient number of samples, demonstrated the greatest success. To the right of these names, in a separate column, were added the names of trainers who had shown enough to make them worth watching closely. They were borderline performers who, in their next few samples, would prove themselves skilled, or simply, lucky.

It was no surprise that several trainers had proven skilled with as many as four Index; a few with three and many with two. Why not? These were the true professionals. It's reasonable they would be skilled in more than one aspect of their training.

On August 28, I was identifying and marking the Index Runners for the next day at Calder when I became excited by something in the first race. The records of the runners made up a handicapper's nightmare and the reason for my excitement appeared equally unreal.

Consider a 4-year-old Maiden filly that never saw the board in 12 races, going for an open $10,000 tag the eighth time competing; and in two of the three previous races, finishing 9th and 5th for $10,500. She shows no workouts and only one recent race. Her margin off the leader in all ten races showing averaged almost 10 lengths, 11-plus lengths in her last 5 races. She beat only 2 of 43 horses out of the gate in her last 4 races. Only one other in the ten-horse field came close to looking so bad;

and all this magnificence being guided today by a 7 lb. apprentice jockey.

None of the *Form* handicappers gave this rose a sniff.

# 1 CALDER

**7 FURLONGS. (1.23⅘) MAIDEN CLAIMING. Purse $4,200. Fillies, 3 and 4-year-olds. Weight, 3-year-olds, 118 lbs. 4-year-olds, 122 lbs. Claiming price $10,000.**

## Sauce Mint
Ch. f. 3, by Sauce Boat—Moments After, by Hasty Flyer
$10,000 Br.—Green Village Investments (Ky)
Tr.—Imprescia Dominic F
118 Lifetime 5 0 0 0 $480 | 1986 3 M 0 0 $480 | 1985 2 M 0 0
Own.—Creek Bend Farm
Entered 27Aug86- 3 CRC

13Aug86- 4Crc fst 7f :23⅕ :47 1:27⅕ 3↑ⒻMd 25000 1 10 94½ 98½ 814 713½ Lester R N 118 7.40 67-15 I'm A Rage 1182 Katie Mac D. 114no Mina Sam 112½ Outrun 10
25Jly86- 1Crc sly 6f :22⅘ :46⅘ 1 14⅖ 3↑ⒻMd 25000 3 10 1017 1016 1013 107½ Lee M A 117 4.60 71-19 Solo Raise 1171½ I'm A Rage 117no Kolorado Kris 110½ Outrun 10
11Jly86- 8Crc fst 6f :22⅘ :46⅘ 1:14⅖ 3↑ⒻMd 40000 4 12 1213 1226 811 57 Lee M A 117 28.20 72-20 HrmonyJig1133½LissCommnd113hdMrs.Prospector118½ No threat 12
11Jly86-Placed fourth through disqualification
6Oct85- 6Bel fst 1 :47⅘ 1:13 1:39 ⒻMd Sp Wt 4 6 95½ 914 926 631½ Santos J A 117 46.10 38-19 Weather Watch117hdPasDesTrois1178MarginalMoney1105 Outrun 9
23Sep85- 5Bel fst 7f :22⅘ :46⅘ 1:25⅘ ⒻMd Sp Wt 3 8 1218 1217 1215 1014½ Thibeau R J 117 51.10 60-25 Whirl Series 1172½ Isn't She Nice 117½ Dr's Nurse 117½ Outrun 12
LATEST WORKOUTS Aug 7 Crc 4f fst :51 b Jly 5 Crc 5f sly 1:03⅕ bg Jun 30 Crc 5f sly 1:02⅕ b

## My Lady Dot
Gr. f. 3, by Always Gallant—Lady Sister, by Saritamer
$10,000 Br.—Delli-Veneri A Jr (Fla)
Tr.—Ubide Max
1117 Lifetime 5 0 0 0 $285 | 1986 5 M 0 0 $285 | 1985 0 M 0 0
Own.—Rolling Oaks Farm

21Aug86- 2Crc fst 1 :49⅘ 1:16 1:43⅕ 3↑ⒻMd 14000 11 9 89½ 811 712 713½ Jawny A7 110 65.20 58-16 Heat Wave 1135 Beach Dancer 106hd Shee Storms 1135 Outrun 12
8Aug86- 3Crc fst 170 :50 1:16⅕ 1:47⅗ 3↑ⒻMd 15000 9 10 95½ 813 817 716 Sarvis D A7 110 71.00 56-18 Serenity Covergirl 1171 Heat Wave 1131 Endless 1171½ Outrun 10
23Jly86-10Crc fst 1 :49⅕ 1:14⅗ 1:41⅘ 3↑ⒻMd 16000 11 11 1213 1119 1123 1119½ Baltazar C 115 41.40 60-17 Pretty Trick 1154½ Visible Rainbow 1152 Heat Wave111hd Outrun 12
11Jly86- 8Crc fst 6f :22⅘ :46⅘ 1:14⅖ 3↑ⒻMd 35000 11 10 1111 1125 1019 914 Baltazar C 113 48.50 65-20 HrmonyJig1133½LissCommnd113hdMrs.Prospector118½ No factor 12
11Jly86-Placed eighth through disqualification
18Jun86- 6Crc fst 6f :22⅘ :47 1:14⅖ 3↑ⒻMd 18000 12 11 1114 1117 710 712 Baltazar C 115 29.00 67-15 Queen Hawaii 1104½ Cash ForDramma1061SprintSail115no Outrun 12
LATEST WORKOUTS Aug 17 Crc 4f sly :49 b ●Aug 4 Crc 5f fst 1:02 b Jly 9 Crc 3f fst :36⅘ b Jly 4 Crc 7f fst 1:31⅘ b

## Terry's Lass
Ch. f. 3, by Amberbee—Lady Leeyan, by Irish Ruler
$10,000 Br.—Bates T (Fla)
Tr.—Bates L
118 Lifetime 3 0 0 0 $137 | 1986 3 M 0 0 $137 | 1985 0 M 0 0
Own.—Bates & Samuels

21Aug86- 2Crc fst 1 :49⅘ 1:16 1:43⅕ 3↑ⒻMd 12000 10 10 1215 1115 1014 916½ Green B 113 15.20 56-16 Heat Wave 1135 Beach Dancer 106hd Shee Storms 1135 Outrun 12
7Aug86- 2Crc fst 6f :22⅕ :46⅘ 1:14⅖ 3↑ⒻMd 10500 9 4 1211 1012 83½ 64½ Green B 114 55.30 74-17 Lcroix'sJulit1144TomhwkPrincss118hdBllsOfHickory118hd Outrun 12
18Jly86- 3Crc fst 6f :22⅘ :46⅖ 1:12⅘ 3↑ⒻMd 10000 7 8 1211 1218 920 717½ Green B 117 66.50 70-17 Forever Secret 11711 Can ThisBe1171TimelessWinter117½ Outrun 12
LATEST WORKOUTS Aug 27 Crc 3f fst :38 bg Jly 15 Crc 3f fst :38 bg Jly 10 Crc 4f fst :51⅘ b Jly 5 Crc 3f sly :38 bg

## I'll Tell Mother
Ch. f. 3, by Superbity—Your Intent, by Bold Hemp
$10,000 Br.—Thornton Joanne & R (Fla)
Tr.—Stirling Kent H
118 Lifetime 6 0 0 0 $727 | 1986 3 M 0 0 $427 | 1985 3 M 0 0 $300
Own.—Thornton Joanne

21Aug86- 2Crc fst 1 :49⅘ 1:16 1:43⅕ 3↑ⒻMd 12000 2 2 11 31½ 48 410 Lee M A 113 6.50 62-16 Heat Wave 1135 Beach Dancer 106hd Shee Storms1135 Weakened 12
7Aug86- 2Crc fst 6f :22⅕ :46⅘ 1:14⅖ 3↑ⒻMd 10500 12 3 64½ 45½ 3nk 44½ •Lee M A 114 57.00 75-17 Lcroix'sJult1144TomhwkPrncss118hdBllsOfHckory118hd Bid, tired 12
24Jly86- 6Crc fst 6f :22⅘ :47⅖ 1:14 3↑ⒻMd 16000 3 9 86½ 99½ 816 1021 Lee M A 117 9.80 60-15 Can This Be 1135½ Moon Kiss 117hd Heavens Love 1077½ Outrun 11
22Jly85- 5Crc sly 6f :21⅘ :46 1:13 ⒻMd 37500 2 5 44½ 58 713 817½ Green B b 115 18.80 68-16 Scotch Threat 1172 Boca Grove 1174 Missy Lutka 1173½ Tired 9
6Jly85- 4Crc fst 5½f :22 :45⅗ 1:06⅕ ⒻMd Sp Wt 7 2 35 412 616 815½ Green B 116 32.30 79-12 Screen Dancer 1162½ Her Honorship 116nk Tea Fortop1161½ Tired 10
29Jun85- 2Crc fst 5½f :23⅗ :48⅕ 1:08⅕ ⒻMd Sp Wt 8 4 43 57½ 811 89½ Green B 115 23.80 74-15 Danza Rustica 115½ Missy Lutka 1151 Fateful Prospect115½ Tired 10
LATEST WORKOUTS Aug 18 Crc 4f fst :49⅘ b Jly 19 Crc 4f fst :51⅘ b Jly 8 Crc 3f fst :37⅘ bg

## Stu's Honey
B. f. 3, by Rollicking—Honey Lil, by Fleet Allied
$10,000 Br.—Brooks & Stautberg & Bogel (Ky)
Tr.—Seiden Stuart
1117 Lifetime 9 0 0 0 $1,155 | 1986 3 M 0 0 $190 | 1985 6 M 0 0 $965
Own.—Millstein & Seiden S & C

23Jly86-10Crc fst 1 :49⅕ 1:14⅗ 1:41⅘ 3↑ⒻMd 16000 8 9 64½ 46 816 918½ Rodriguez E M 115 33.20 60-17 Pretty Trick 1154½ Visible Rainbow 1152 Heat Wave 111hd Tired 12
16Jly86- 6Crc fst 6f :22⅗ :47⅕ 1:14 3↑ⒻMd 20000 5 10 127½ 1111 911 711½ Rodriguez E M 117 4.90 69-19 That's A Good One 1174½ Rhonda's Ring117noBabbsie117½ Outrun 12
25Jun86- 7Crc fst 6f :22⅕ :46⅕ 1:14 3↑ⒻMd 35000 9 2 77½ 815 714 77½ Gunther S F7 108 37.10 74-17 Rezumbante 120no Call Doctor Barry 1151 Richie 1151 Outrun 9
9Dec85- 1Crc fst 170 :50⅘ 1:16⅘ 1:47⅘ ⒻMd 35000 5 2 2½ 33 511 517½ Pennisi F A 120 8.80 53-17 Raspberry Beret 1207 Darby Del 1112½ Turveil 120½ Tired 8
29Nov85-10Crc fst 1 :49⅗ 1.15⅗ 1:43⅕ ⒻMd 40000 4 2 2hd 31 58½ 614½ Pennisi F A 119 24.60 57-16 Valkyrie 115½ Raspberry Beret 115nk Darby Del 110½ Tired 9
17Jly85- 3Crc fst 6f :22⅘ :46⅗ 1:12⅘ ⒻMd 70000 7 2 63½ 712 79½ 612½ Russ M L 113 5.30 74-13 Portio 1176½ Dustagal 117no Coequal 1172 Outrun 8
10Jly85- 3Crc fst 6f :22⅗ :46⅗ 1:12⅘ ⒻMd Sp Wt 6 1 56 45½ 58 814 Velez J A Jr 116 19.30 75-12 Top Folly 1168½ Rainy Gal 1161 Missy Lutka 1162 Tired 8
29Jun85- 2Crc fst 5½f :23⅗ :48⅕ 1.08⅕ ⒻMd Sp Wt 2 8 87½ 810 79 76½ Velez J A Jr 115 9.50 77-15 Danza Rustica 115½ Missy Lutka 1151FatefulProspect115½ Outrun 10
12Jun85- 6Crc fst 5f :23 :48 1.00⅘ ⒻMd 50000 5 6 117½ 109½ 67½ 45½ Russ M L 116 24.00 83-16 Raise A Duchess 1163NakedThoughts113½Sagadahoc1161½ Rallied 11
LATEST WORKOUTS Jly 12 Crc 4f sly :50⅘ b Jly 5 Crc 5f sly 1:03⅘ b

## Miss Knight Bars
Dk. b. or br. f. 3, by Holme In Dark—Rambling True, by True Knight
$10,000 Br.—Strickland M C (Fla)
Tr.—Jordan Donald
118 Lifetime 4 0 0 0 $630 | 1986 4 M 0 0 $630 | 1985 0 M 0 0
Own.—Strickland M C

1Aug86- 4Crc fst 6f :22⅕ :45⅘ 1:13⅗ 3↑ⒻMd 20000 11 1 22½ 413 1026 1029 Green B b 118 144.00 54-14 Flair For It 1185½ Babbsie 118hd Richie 118hd Stopped 11
11Jly86- 8Crc fst 6f :22⅘ :46⅘ 1:14⅖ 3↑ⒻMd 35000 12 4 109½ 1024 1228 1232½ Suckie M C b 113 109.90 47-20 HarmonyJig1133½LisasCommand113hdMrs.Prospector118½ Outrun 12
11Jly86-Placed eleventh through disqualification
11Jun86- 6Crc fst 6f :22⅘ :46⅗ 1:13⅘ 3↑ⒻMd 40000 7 4 21½ 711 1024 1032½ Suckie M C b 115 17.50 49-14 Golden Afternoon 1063½ Rezumbante 1181½ Richie115½ Early foot 10
27May86- 6Hia fst 6f :22⅕ :46⅗ 1:12⅗ 3↑ Md 35000 4 2 31 1½ 510 419 Suckie M C b 108 14.90 58-23 Mister N. J. G.1113½ShearSteel113½Dancer'sFunnyface12215 Tired 7

## Galloping Gal
Dk. b. or br. f. 3, by Infusion—Fretful Gal, by Restless Native
$10,000 Br.—Pollack I (Ky)
Tr.—Decosta Vivianne
118 Lifetime 14 0 0 0 $1,330 | 1986 6 M 0 0 $350 | 1985 8 M 0 0 $980
Own.—Peacefulridge Farm

21Aug86- 2Crc fst 1 :49⅘ 1:16 1:43⅕ 3↑ⒻMd 12000 4 1 21 56 612 813½ Bain G W 114 60.20 58-16 Heat Wave 1135 Beach Dancer 106hd Shee Storms 1135 Tired 12
8Aug86- 3Crc fst 170 :50 1:16⅕ 1:47⅗ 3↑ⒻMd 14000 7 6 74½ 710 713 610½ Astorga C 115 57.30 61-18 Serenity Covergirl 1171 Heat Wave 1131 Endless 1171½ No threat 10
1Aug86- 4Crc fst 6f :22⅕ :45⅘ 1:13⅗ 3↑ⒻMd 18000 2 9 912 921 714 69½ Astorga C 114 199.00 73-14 Flair For It 1185½ Babbsie 118hd Richie 118hd Outrun 11
23Jly86-10Crc fst 1 :49⅕ 1:14⅗ 1:41⅘ 3↑ⒻMd 16000 12 7 75 915 1020 1018½ Paynter L A7 108 161.70 60-17 Pretty Trick 1154½ Visible Rainbow 1152 Heat Wave111hd Outrun 12
3Jly86- 6Crc fst 6f :22⅗ 47⅕ 1.12⅘ 3↑ⒻMd 20000 4 12 1217 1219 1114 1014½ Astorga C 114 106.50 73-16 Gonna Skate 1133½RuleofThree117noThat'sAGoodOne1175 Outrun 12
20Jun86-10Crc sly 7f :23⅗ :47⅕ 1:27⅘ 3↑ⒻMd 25000 11 2 2hd 84½ 1019 913½ Astorga C b 114 37.70 66-15 DustyGal1141½LisasCommnd1141SerenityCovergirl114½ Brief foot 12
23Sep85- 6Crc fst 170 :49⅘ 1:15⅗ 1:48⅘ ⒻMd 18000 1 2 46 712 918 920½ Philpot E7 b 107 49.30 47-17 Mississippi Jig 1149½ This Is Talent1142½Vagueness1181½ Stopped 9
9Sep85- 3Crc fst 1 :49⅗ 1:15⅘ 1:43⅕ ⒻMd 20000 2 1 3½ 58 416 423½ Fackler T10 b 107 16.10 49-18 Fast Frills 1188½ Mississippi Jig 11810 This Is Talent 1184½ Tired 7
29Aug85-10Crc fst 7f :23 :47⅕ 1.28⅘ ⒻMd 30000 4 9 87½ 911 1024 1013½ Bain G W b 114 61.20 60-18 Kadoba 1144½ Bold Aloha 116½ Flashy Ann 118½ Outrun 12
23Aug85- 6Crc fst 6f :22⅕ :46⅗ 1:14⅖ ⒻMd 18000 3 11 1216 1017 98½ 77½ Squartino R A b 114 26.30 71-13 SprinkleofRine118½FlyingBirdie1182½MississippiJig1183 No factor 12

## Tudor Jours
Ro. f. 4, by Tudor Gleeman—Lady Redfern, by Royal Award
$10,000 Br.—Shuford Nancy C (Ky)
Tr.—Tammaro John
1157 Lifetime 12 0 0 0 $1,007 | 1986 6 M 0 0 $467 | 1985 6 M 0 0 $540
Own.—Lee D L

21Aug86- 2Crc fst 1 :49⅘ 1.16 1:43⅕ 3↑ⒻMd 14000 7 11 1013 913 812 613½ Molina V H 122 11.50 58-16 Heat Wave 1135 Beach Dancer 106hd Shee Storms 1135 Outrun 12
10Jly86- 4Crc fst 7f :22⅘ :46⅘ 1:28⅕ 3↑ⒻMd 10500 12 12 1112 1013 1011 98½ Nunez E O5 113 11.20 66-18 Darby Del 110½ Bouncing Shellie 1171 Lee'sNicetime106no Outrun 12
20Jun86- 4Crc fst 6f :22⅘ :47 1:14⅗ 3↑ⒻMd 10500 6 12 128½ 1011 67 53½ Nunez E O5 114 14.30 75-15 MrkdEncountr112hdBllsOfHickory1162BouncngShll116hd Late bid 12
27May86- 2Hia fst 6f :22⅘ :46⅗ 1:13 3↑ⒻMd 12500 11 10 1013 916 611 411½ Nunez E O5 117 27.70 63-23 SurfceMissile1139½IndinSummrBug1131½PrttyAndWis113½ Outrun 11
14May86- 1Hia fst 1⅛ :47⅕ 1.14 1:54⅘ 3↑ Md 10000 7 7 619 616 518 518½ Marty A7 110 14.90 41-22 ⒹOrco 1131½ Another Libra 108½ English Cliffe 11316 No factor 8
11May86- 4Hia fst 6f :23⅕ :46⅗ 1.13 3↑ⒻMd 10000 5 7 86 814 715 611½ Lee M A 122 13.20 64-24 GoldBadge113noIndinSummerBug1064ExuberntJne1137 No factor 9
20Jun85- 6Crc gd 1 :48⅘ 1.14⅗ 1:43⅘ 3↑ⒻMd 13000 2 2 33 76½ 1015 1217½ Velez J A Jr 112 5.30 53-18 DHTQY114DHWckdQn107½Btty sBrthdy1143½ Fin after one half 12
13Jun85- 4Crc fst 7f :23 :47⅘ 1 27⅗ 3↑ⒻMd 10000 10 2 63 54½ 47 68½ Velez J A Jr 115 8.30 70-14 Wings of Love 1151½ Te Qui Yaw 115nk CentralRole1151 Checked 12
20Mar85- 4Crc fst 7f :23⅘ :47⅘ 1:29⅘ 3↑ⒻMd 10000 6 5 63½ 74 56 44½ Santos J A 115 3.00 65-19 Undercover 115½ Aku Dancer 115½ Satan's Triangle 1102½ Rallied 11
10Mar85- 2Crc fst 6f :22⅕ :46⅕ 1 15 3↑ⒻMd 10000 5 10 108½ 512 57½ 42 Santos J A 114 9.70 74-15 Too Available 114hd Rozmon 114no Dart's Pleasure 1092 Steadied 12

**Assured Lady** Gr. f. 3, by Iron Ruler—Marquestian, by Chieftain
Own.—Maplewood Stable $10,000 Br.—Combest R M (Fla) Tr.—Warren Fred G 118
Lifetime 8 0 0 0 $844 1986 8 M 0 0 $844 1985 0 M 0 0

21Aug86- 2Crc fst 1 :49⅘ 1:16 1:43⅕ 3+ ⒻMd 12000 1 3 44½ 66½ 59½ 512 Sarvis D A7 b 106 11.80 60-16 Heat Wave 1135 Beach Dancer 106no Shee Storms 1135 Fell back 12
15Aug86- 1Crc fst 6f :22⅘ 46⅘ 1:14 3+ ⒻMd 10000 12 3 84 56 56½ 55½ Pezua J M b 118 22.40 76-18 TimelessWinter118-KnewYouWhen1082½BchDncr111no No factor 12
24Jly86- 6Crc fst 6f :22⅘ 47⅘ 1:14 3+ ⒻMd 14000 8 7 96½ 66½ 46½ 413 Lester R N b 113 4.80 68-15 Can This Be 1135½ Moon Kiss 117no Heavens Love 1077½ Rallied 11
10Jly86- 4Crc fst 7f :22⅘ 46⅘ 1:28⅕ 3+ ⒻMd 12500 3 8 77½ 77½ 99 109½ Lester R N b 117 4.80 65-18 Darby Del 110½ Bouncing Shellie 1171 Lee'sNicetime106no Outrun 12
2Jly86- 1Crc sly 6f :22⅕ 47 1:15 3+ ⒻMd c-10000 8 12 119 710 21 42½ Suckie M C b 117 7.10 74-19 VisionLdy117½TomhwkPrincess110noDncingNurse1171½ Bid, hung 12
26Jun86- 6Crc fst 7f :23 46⅘ 1:27⅕ 3+ ⒻMd 15000 7 5 52½ 45½ 67½ 611½ Suckie M C b 115 8.60 68-18 Hope For Best 1152 Darby Del 1081½ PrettyTrick1152½ Weakened 12
18Jun86- 6Crc fst 6f :22⅘ 47 1:14⅘ 3+ ⒻMd 18000 7 10 109½ 78½ 43 45½ Suckie M C b 115 16.50 73-15 QueenHawaii1104½CashForDramma1061SprintSail115no No threat 12
25Apr86- 3Hia fst 6f :22⅘ 46⅘ 1:13⅘ 3+ ⒻMd 20000 6 10 1014 1016 1016 912 Baltazar C b 113 29.40 60-22 GenuinelyGold124½BenignBegum1261Deborh'sPlesur1191½ Outrun 10
LATEST WORKOUTS Aug 13 Crc 4f sly :51⅕ b Aug 8 Crc 6f fst 1:17⅘ b Aug 3 Crc 3f fst :39 b Jly 22 Crc 3f fst :36 b

~~**Vienna Landing**~~ SCR Dk. b. or br. f. 3, by Seventh Landing—Vienna Queen, by Ambler
Own.—DuBois R M $10,000 Br.—McRary D A (Tex) Tr.—Thomas Emery E 118
Lifetime 4 0 0 0 $143 1986 3 M 0 0 $103 1985 1 M 0 0 $40

31Jan86- 1Tam fst 7f :23⅕ 46⅘ 1:27 ⒻMd 6500 9 9 89½ 710 99½ 913½ Gomez J I b 114 33.10 75-14 Silver Speed 118no Lee's Nicetime 118½ Oxford's Joy 1182 Outrun 10
24Jan86- 7Tam fst 7f :23 46⅘ 1:26⅘ ⒻMd Sp Wt 5 6 78 812 810 718 Gomez J I 118 59.20 74-15 DropMeaLine1188AlwaysWishing118½ClassicAndRoyl1113 Outrun 10
3Jan86- 4Crc fst 6f :22⅘ 46⅘ 1:13⅘ ⒻMd 12500 6 8 106½ 812 912 813½ Lynch H D 120 122.90 68-18 Forever Flower 1152 Solaton 1207½ Last Citation 1201½ No factor 12
27Dec85- 1Crc fst 7f :23⅕ 47⅘ 1:27⅘ ⒻMd 12500 12 7 1113 1214 1115 1017 Paynter L A5 115 82.50 62-16 ForeverRoving1204½MyMoodyDebs1151½LndofthBold1201 Outrun 12
LATEST WORKOUTS Aug 20 Crc 5f fst 1:04 b Aug 14 Crc 3f fst :37 b Aug 8 Crc 5f fst 1:05 bg

**Miss Restivo** Dk. b. or br. f. 3, by Restivo—Oh Missie, by Oh Johnny
Own.—Paulisin Delores & P $10,000 Br.—Griffis E E (Fla) Tr.—Azpurua Manuel J 118
Lifetime 14 0 0 1 $1,520 1986 9 M 0 1 $1,055 1985 5 M 0 0 $465

8Aug86- 3Crc fst 170 :50 1:16⅕ 1:47⅘ 3+ ⒻMd 13000 2 9 85½ 914 920 918½ Pezua J M b 113 13.80 53-18 Serenity Covergirl 1171 Heat Wave 1131 Endless 1171½ Outrun 10
30Jly86- 1Crc fst 7f :22⅘ 46⅘ 1:28⅘ 3+ ⒻMd 10000 10 1 910 813 812 79 Prado E S b 117 19.30 63-17 BouncingShellie117ⒹKnewYouWhen1102½HevnsLov107½ Outrun 12
24Apr86- 3Hia fst 1⅛ :49⅗ 1:16 1:57⅘ 3+ ⒻMd 12500 3 5 57½ 57½ 44 44 Jawny A5 b 107 9.10 41-30 EtTuChief1182PlesntCtch1171½NoRoomAtTheInn112½ Drifted out 6
14Apr86- 1Hia fst 1⅛ 48⅘ 1:15⅕ 1:54⅗ 3+ ⒻMd 12500 2 4 42½ 2hd 48½ 412½ Suckie M C5 b 107 6.80 46-20 Trickston 11210 Pleasant Catch 122no Play Cards 1122½ Bid, tired 7
27Mar86- 7Tam fst 1 1/16 48⅘ 1:14⅘ 1:48⅘ ⒻMd 6300 7 8 811 711 59 35½ Alexander T C b 112 23.10 70-18 Compiler 1184 Amusive 1121½ Miss Restivo 112½ Rallied 8
20Mar86- 3Tam fst 7f :23⅘ 47 1:28⅕ ⒻMd 5000 2 9 912 911 65 56½ Whitley K b 118 18.40 76-16 SmplyFn118noOxford'sJoy1185FshnMFrnch1181½ Shuffled bk. st. 10
27Feb86- 4Tam fst 6f :22⅘ 47 1:14⅘ ⒻMd 5000 1 12 129½ 1211 107½ 85½ Whitley K b 118 45.50 68-20 RisingTheStkes111noLikeAnAngel118½Demonsqu'sPt1091½ Outrun 12
11Feb86- 4Tam sly 7f :24 46⅘ 1:28⅘ ⒻMd 5000 7 9 810 812 1016 1024 Londono O A b 118 12.70 56-24 Celines Kriss 1188 Gofore Logic 1111½ Wide Mission1181½ Outrun 10
3Jan86- 1Crc fst 6f :22⅘ 47 1:14⅕ ⒻMd 12500 9 8 1113 1218 1116 914 Lauzon J M b 120 64.00 66-18 Chenessa 120hd Flight North 1202½ Regal Majesty 120hd Outrun 12

Consensus Totals Based on 5 points for First (7 for Best Bet), 2 for 2nd 1 for 3rd. Best Bet in **Bold Type. Reigh Count selections not included in Consensus.**

| | TRACKMAN | HANDICAP | ANALYST | HERMIS | SWEEP | REIGH COUNT | CONSENSUS | |
|---|---|---|---|---|---|---|---|---|
| 1 | Sauce Mint | I'll Tell Mother | Sauce Mint | Sauce Mint | I'll Tell Mother | Sauce Mint | Sauce Mint | 15 |
| | Assured Lady | Assured Lady | I'll Tell Mother | Stu's Honey | Assured Lady | Stu's Honey | I'll Tell Mother | 14 |
| | I'll Tell Mother | Stu's Honey | Miss Restivo | I'll Tell Mother | Tudor Jours | Assured Lady | Assured Lady | 6 |
| 2 | Turkish Toast | **M. S Wig** | **Miss Toasty** | Miss Toasty | Miss Toasty | M S Wig | Miss Toasty | 19 |
| | M S Wig | Miss Toasty | M S Wig | M S. Wig | M S Wig | Turkish Toast | M S. Wig | 15 |
| | Bates Road | Sevna | Turkish Toast | Turkish Toast | Turkish Toast | Golden Greens | Turkish Toast | 8 |
| 3 | Above Gossip | Miss Lady Luck | Miss Lady Luck | Miss Lady Luck | Pajaro Gris | Sayonara Silver | Miss Lady Luck | 16 |
| | Super Dee | Screamin Tanthem | Pajaro Gris | Pajaro Gris | Screamin Tanthem | Super Dee | Pajaro Gris | 9 |
| | Sayonara Silver | Indywood | Indywood | Above Gossip | Miss Lady Luck | Screamin Tanthem | Above Gossip | 6 |
| 4 | Nanas Secretary | Swoonski | Cast a Lot | Cast a Lot | Pick's Story | Nanas Secretary | Cast a Lot | 14 |
| | Vacillating Steve | Cast a Lot | Swoonski | Striking Haven | Cast a Lot | Cast a Lot | Pick's Story | 8 |
| | Reckless Blue | Pick's Story | Pick's Story | Pick's Story | Striking Haven | Pick's Story | Swoonski | 7 |
| 5 | Annie Blueeyes | Golden Actress | Annie Blueeyes | Annie Blueeyes | Hermeda | **Annie Blueeyes** | Annie Blueeyes | 18 |
| | Alan's Gal | Annie Blueeyes | Golden Actress | Golden Actress | Alan's Gal | Hermeda | Golden Actress | 9 |
| | Hermeda | Alan's Gal | Hermeda | Hermeda | Annie Blueeyes | Too Darned Hot | Hermeda | 8 |
| 6 | Flying Mac | Icepasser | Flying Mac | **Icepasser** | **Icepasser** | Legal Lassie | Icepasser | 21 |
| | Riada | Flying Mac | Icepasser | Riada | Riada | Flying Mac | Flying Mac | 14 |
| | Slide Forward | Riada | Passport to Riches | Flying Mac | Flying Mac | Catchy Blonde | Riada | 7 |
| 7 | Homo Adonis | Olympus | River Rage | Olympus | Olympus | Anyone's Guess | Olympus | 15 |
| | Okie Osage | Okie Osage | Anyone's Guess | Double Scribe | River Rage | Okie Osage | River Rage | 8 |
| | Double Scribe | River Rage | Double Scribe | Anyone's Guess | Double Scribe | Double Scribe | Homo Adonis | 5 |
| 8 | Doctor's Echo | Go Ask Dad | Go Ask Dad | Go Ask Dad | Go Ask Dad | Strong Beat | **Go Ask Dad** | 21 |
| | Kindly Court | Doctor's Echo | He's So Neat | Kindly Court | Inside Tip | Sunshine Bear | Doctor's Echo | 7 |
| | Go Ask Dad | Big Prediction | Lord Pro | Nitaforever | Kindly Court | Coro Pro | Kindly Court | 5 |
| 9 | **Res Ipsa** | Medieval Iron | Parting Words | Res Ipsa | Res Ipsa | Medieval Iron | Res Ipsa | 17 |
| | Medieval Iron | Parting Words | Medieval Iron | Autistic | Parting Words | Res Ipsa | Parting Words | 10 |
| | Autistic | Overage | Expansive | Parting Words | Autistic | Expansive | Medieval Iron | 9 |
| 10 | Ell's Dusty Lark | La Mala | Ell's Dusty Lark | Dinner With Diane | Ell's Dusty Lark | La Mala | Ell's Dusty Lark | 17 |
| | Dinner With Diane | Zindian | La Mala | Ell's Dusty Lark | La Mala | Zindian | La Mala | 11 |
| | La Mala | Dark Rumor | Vision Lady | La Mala | Wicked Queen | Dark Rumor | Dinner With Diane | 7 |

**FIRST RACE**                                    *Probable Post, 1:30*
7 FURLONGS. 3 & 4–Year–Olds. Maidens Claiming ($10,000). Purse $4,200.

| P.P. | Horse | Pr.Rider. | Wt. | Comment. | Pr.Odds. |
|------|-------|-----------|-----|----------|----------|
| 1 | SAUCE MINT | Lester R N | 118 | Maybe with these | 5-2 |
| 5 | STU'S HONEY | Paynter L A | 7111 | Drops; may contend | 3-1 |
| 4 | I'LL TELL MOTHER | Lee M A | 118 | Merits consideration | 4-1 |
| 8 | TUDOR JOURS | Sarvis D A | 7115 | Some late foot | 8-1 |
| 9 | ASSURED LADY | Smith A Jr | 118 | Chance for part | 10-1 |
| 11 | MISS RESTIVO | Perez E O | 118 | Must show more | 2-1 |
| 6 | MISS KNIGHT BARS | Green B | 118 | Never close | 15-1 |
| 2 | MY LADY DOT | Jawny A | 7111 | Lacks speed | 15-1 |
| 3 | TERRY'S LASS | Green B | 118 | Doesn't figure | 15-1 |
| 7 | GALLOPING GAL | Bain G W | 118 | Usually far back | 20-1 |
| 10 | VIENNA LANDING | No Rider | 118 | Outrun vs softer | 20-1 |

Blinkers On: Sauce Mint, Terry's Lass.

The reason for my excitement which had me wringing my hands, Tudor Jours qualified under not one, but two Index where John Tammaro had already proven his ability to succeed, "Fastback" and "Route to 7 furlongs" (FBK and Rt7). He had a high percentage of success in both these situations.

Tammaro, under any condition is somebody to respect. Tammaro, under a proven Index is found money. Tammaro, under two proven Index cost me a lot of sleep the night before. This was the first time a horse had come up under two Index, both proven by the trainer. I bet his horse with enthusiasm.

The ease with which Tudor Jours won this race is one of the brighter nuggets of reinforcement for handicapping trainers. The sad part of this race was that the price of 9 to 1 would have been twice that had the horse not been the only 4-year-old in a field of 3-year-olds.

**FIRST RACE** 7 FURLONGS. (1.23⅕) MAIDEN CLAIMING. Purse $4,200. Fillies, 3 and 4-year-olds. Weight, 3-year-olds, 118 lbs. 4-year-olds, 122 lbs. Claimng price $10,000. (106th Day. WEATHER CLEAR. TEMPERATURE 89 DEGREES.)

**Calder**

AUGUST 29

**Value of race $4,200; value to winner $2,520; second $756; third $462; fourth $210; balance of starters $42 each. Mutuel pool $20,831.**

| Last Raced | Horse | Eqt. | A. | Wt | PP | St | ¼ | ½ | Str | Fin | Jockey | Cl'g Pr | Odds $1 |
|---|---|---|---|---|---|---|---|---|---|---|---|---|---|
| 21Aug86 2Crc6 | Tudor Jours | | 4 | 115 | 8 | 10 | 81 | 6½ | 1½ | 11¼ | Sarvis D A7 | 10000 | 8.70 |
| 23Jly86 10Crc9 | Stu's Honey | | 3 | 111 | 5 | 5 | 5hd | 5hd | 4½ | 2½ | Paynter L A7 | 10000 | 6.80 |
| 21Aug86 2Crc4 | I'll Tell Mother | | 3 | 118 | 4 | 3 | 3hd | 3½ | 54 | 31½ | Lee M A | 10000 | 2.70 |
| 21Aug86 2Crc8 | Galloping Gal | | 3 | 118 | 7 | 1 | 21 | 2hd | 2hd | 4no | Fackler T | 10000 | 17.60 |
| 13Aug86 4Crc7 | Sauce Mint | b | 3 | 118 | 1 | 4 | 44 | 44 | 3hd | 52½ | Lester R N | 10000 | 1.70 |
| 21Aug86 2Crc9 | Terry's Lass | b | 3 | 118 | 3 | 9 | 71½ | 10 | 7½ | 6¾ | Hernandez C | 10000 | 21.60 |
| 21Aug86 2Crc5 | Assured Lady | b | 3 | 118 | 9 | 8 | 91 | 83 | 62 | 7nk | Smith A Jr | 10000 | 4.90 |
| 21Aug86 2Crc7 | My Lady Dot | | 3 | 111 | 2 | 6 | 6½ | 71½ | 81 | 8nk | Jawny A7 | 10000 | 50.60 |
| 8Aug86 3Crc9 | Miss Restivo | b | 3 | 118 | 10 | 7 | 10 | 9hd | 94 | 95 | Perez O E | 10000 | 33.60 |
| 1Aug86 4Crc10 | Miss Knight Bars | b | 3 | 118 | 6 | 2 | 14 | 14 | 10 | 10 | Green B | 10000 | 20.00 |

**OFF AT 1:02; Start good, Won driving. Time, :23, :47⅕, 1:14⅘, 1:28⅘ Track fast.**

**Official Program Numbers**

| **$2 Mutuel Prices:** | | | |
|---|---|---|---|
| 8-TUDOR JOURS | 19.40 | 7.60 | 3.60 |
| 5-STU'S HONEY | | 7.20 | 4.60 |
| 4-I'LL TELL MOTHER | | | 3.20 |

**Ro. f, by Tudor Gleeman—Lady Redfern, by Royal Award. Trainer Tammaro John. Bred by Shuford Nancy C (Ky).**

TUDOR JOURS slowest to begin, rallied along the outside in the drive, gained command in midstretch and was clear at the finish. STU'S HONEY in hand early, was inside for the stretch run, was on even terms with the winner in midstretch, but was outfinishd. I'LL TELL MOTHER raced forwardly, could not gain ground in the final eighth. GALOPING GAL raced in the attending position, reached even terms for command in midstretch, but could not sustain the bid. SAUCE MINT raced forwardly, joined the leaders in midstretch, but had little left. ASSURED LADY was outrun. MISS KNIGHT BARS set the pace to the head of the stretch, then weakened.

**Owners**— 1, Lee D L; 2, Millstein & Seiden S & C; 3, Tiorrnton Joanne; 4, Peacefulridge Farm; 5, Creek Bend Farm; 6, Bates & Samuels; 7, Maplewood Stable; 8, Rolling Oaks Farm; 9, Paulisin Delores & P; 10, Strickland M C.

**Trainers**— 1, Tammaro John; 2, Seiden Stuart; 3, Stirling Kent H; 4, Decosta Vivianne; 5, Imprescia Dominic F; 6, Bates L; 7, Warren Fred G; 8, Ubide Max; 9, Azpurua Manuel J; 10, Jordan Donald.

**Scratched**—Vienna Landing (31Jan86 1Tam9).



There are some genius horsemen out there and most never make the top ten. This is strongly evident when tracking the history of the top claiming trainers. They have an eye for some fault in another's horse; something they know how to fix. It could be something the horse is getting too much (or too little) of in his diet or exercise program. It could be as small a thing as the wrong shoes.

They claim the horse, change what needs to be changed, and are back on the track with an "up in class" surprise for anyone who doesn't know of their talent.

There could be no profit on these professionals if it were not for all the trainers who claim horses and drive them right down the tubes. The same can be said for the other high visibility situations; First Time Starters, Routers dropping back to 7 furlongs. The large number of failing attempts tends to obscure the 1 out of 30 who knows what he's doing. It takes some digging to learn the names.

**Time to Coast**

My handicapping, in the most conventional sense, was finished. These professionals had spent most of their lives learning how to do it for me. All I had to do now was wait for the Index to show up. It might appear:

"Alexander, Frank L-3 entered at 1 mile on the Turf."

"Romero, Jorge FTS A 4 year-old going around 2 turns."

"Ferriola, Peter Cl-1 for Riccio."

"Tammaro, John Rt7Far back last time out around two
                turns; today in for 7 furlongs..."

...and others. I didn't have to think beyond that. I didn't have to look at the rest of the field or the handicappers selections, the jockey, the tote board or the warmup. These proven professionals had already done all of that for me, simply by knowing where and when to enter their horse. I became their silent partner. All I had to do was get my money down. They had done all the work connected with handicapping. The betting became automatic.

Instead of spending hours in ambivalence, pouring over the *Racing Form*, that time was spent identifying the Index Runners and getting them into my files, to be updated after the results were in. Maintaining the records is nearly all of the work left for me. Whenever I record a winner in a trainer's file, I have the chance to reexamine it right there and then to see if this win brings him into that select group I bet automatically. Recording losers only verifies what I've learned already; but it has to be kept up.

Each passing month left behind an incredible amount of new information; fresh information on every trainer who ran a horse in any of the Index situations that were being recorded. If there is a new trainer in town, he would be in the file before the horse catches his breath. From that point, all of his activity will be followed up to the time conclusions can be drawn. He's either a winner, or just another one of the also-rans.

Having a license to train horses is no proof he or she has whatever it takes to produce success. A driver's license is testimony to one's ability to operate a machine. One can, or one can not. On the other hand, a hunting license is testimony to nothing related to putting food on the table, but merely a legal authorization to try. The percentage of hunters coming home empty is probably close to the number of horse trainers who couldn't find the winners circle with Calumet's finest. Call it what you like; luck (or rather, the lack of luck), ignorance, fate, it really doesn't matter. Incompetents exist and they always will.

Along the way, our records point out who they are. That done, we can be grateful for them. Their unfortunate charges take a good share of the betting activity away from our choice. If only the competent were allowed to participate, we'd soon be bored with 3-horse races and $2.40 payoffs.

It's as important to know who can not get the job done as it is to know who can. Even the least able will sometimes find the winners circle and those situations can incorporate the lion's share of whatever can be called, "racing luck." These unpredictable wins will ruin the best laid plans, but that's nothing new to a horseplayer. No need to rattle. The competent trainers will produce more than enough to wipe out the occasional surprise by their less-talented colleagues.

All the lists purporting to identify the top trainers use "number of wins" and "total purses won" as the yardstick of success, permitting trainers of large stables to be included by sheer force of numbers. This is unfair to the many skilled trainers who can not afford to keep "buying" until a winner turns up.

It is our purpose to take advantage of it. The more misleading information floating around out there, the better for anybody who will go the extra mile to learn the facts. Many of the most competent never make these lists and we should be glad of it. Let them stay under wraps, coming from nowhere and paying 10-to-1 and up.

There are times a professional gets *too good*.

Bringing in a lot of winners is great for the trainers and owners, but not for trainer handicappers. In Maryland, Ronald Alfano, Dale Capuano and Thomas Caviness have a great way with horses recently claimed but they've been to the well so often it's hard to get a decent price on them now.

John Tammaro experienced the same problem in Florida. His Carolsteve claims were so consistent (so many of them) even the watchers from Holiday Inn were catching on. After "Hopedale O" on September 11, I had to settle for a lot less than I was used to. Oscar Barrera, John Lenzini, Jr., and Gaspar Moschera brought the same thing on themselves in New York. They got too good too often in this highly visible situation.

This does not mean your research on these men is no longer useful. It means you have to search a little deeper. It isn't a problem if you have the information.

## What's Happening Here?

It probably occurred to you, somewhere in these later pages, that with this approach, we are no longer betting horses. The horse would be all but out of the picture; merely a tool in the hands of a man. The horse will do what the man has trained it to do. The time is chosen by the man; the money is on The Man.

Examining today's *Racing Form*, we're not looking at horses. We're looking down the center of the column at trainer names, and we keep going until a name rings a bell; "Alexander, Frank." Even then we don't look at the horse. We jump up to the Distance and Track Surface; then, if it's 7 furlongs or more or on the Turf, our eyes go to the Date of the last race, hoping it was 2 or 3 months ago. No. Only twelve days. Our eye passes on to the next trainer's name; and the next until the bell rings again.

We're looking for one of the trainers on our list who is running a horse today in the Index he has proven himself competent. Only then do we have a bet, but the bet is not on the horse. It's on the trainer to continue his demonstration of expertise.

He may not win today; but he doesn't have to. He only has to run another horse in this same Index later, tomorrow, next week. He only has to keep entering his horses in this special situation. The wins will come, he's already proven that. We don't want too many wins. That draws attention; destroys the price. Win just enough to maintain the profit.

We don't know when he will choose to do it, or with what horse. We only know he will. We can't afford to assume his intentions today; he's getting that price because he's able to fool the bettors. He can fool us too. We don't have to run that risk. We can be 95% sure of a profit if we simply get there with our $2 every time he runs his Index. We must try not to miss him.

Not only do we want to be there every time; we have to make the same bet each time. $2, $20; $100. It has to be the same every time. If not, Murphy (if anything can go wrong, it will) will see to it your $50's all go on the losers and when the winner gets in you'll be holding a $20 ticket. You can count on this. There are proper times to raise or lower a bet. Trying to out-guess the man is not one of the criteria.

This is not horsebetting. We're investing in a skilled professional's proven ability to get a particular done. This isn't somebody we picked off the boat. We already put him to the test. He's proven his skill and is worthy of our faith in him. He's now doing all the work; we're just along for the ride. Our work was done after we pulled him out of that sea of numbers. Now we just wait for him to do the thing we know he can, in his own time.

In Chapter One it was mentioned that conventional handicapping techniques never reach a point where we can lay back and coast. As long as we stay in the game, the pressure is constant. There is no relief from this. A race is over and we win or lose. The next race is off in 25 minutes. Again, it's win or lose and no relief of pressure.

Using this approach dissolves that pressure completely. The hardest part of the job is gathering the data to learn who could do what. After we have it, it doesn't change from race to race, day to day, or even month to month.

When a Pro gets good at something he doesn't use it once, then disappear in smoke. In most cases it goes on for years, unseen, unheralded, known only to himself and the masochist who tracked him down.

The pressure is off because we already found our winner in the man. He doesn't have to put the horse over today. A win today might mean four, five or six losers coming up in the weeks ahead. It doesn't matter when the win comes. When his horse finishes fifth our money is not lost. We were not betting on the horse but on the man. Our time to cash in is down the line. This will sound incredible but, when the horse loses, we learn not to care. Have you ever felt *that* before?

Is this approach right for you? Only you can answer that. But, regardless of how your new knowledge is used, you will be further ahead than if you ignore it altogether. It's too *powerful* to be ignored!

CHAPTER NINE

# Race-Search, Inc.

# Race-Search, Inc.

Florida winter racing becomes something quite different from the rest of the year so, in June of the same year, I began getting ready for it by coding Belmont, Pimlico, and Monmouth Park along with Calder. With what I charted the winter past, I would have a very good line on shippers as they arrived. However, two unexpected events conspired to turn that coming season in a different direction.

My files on northern trainers were just beginning to be worthwhile when *Daily Racing Form* cut off the information supply. In October, they stopped freighting the papers from Hightstown and got a Pompano firm to print a Florida Advance Edition from films sent by satellite. Those films no longer included any northern racing with the exception of whatever New York track was running. Florida patrons were now offered an ink-smeared edition of less than half it's previous volume. The price, of course, remained the same.

The second event was the unexpected sale (on December 1) of the house in which I was living. This had me working out of boxes and from the back of my car for a period that stretched into February. As long as I was uprooted, I didn't want to commit to a new lease until I was sure of the best location for my plans, and Florida was not looking good.

At this time I made several inquiries, hoping to speed up my data intake of trainer information. Mr. Williams at the *Racing Form* was not unwilling, but explained they kept only enough information in their computers to print their papers, and suggested I contact Bloodstock Research in Kentucky. After looking at my requirements, Mr. Faust told me they were coming out with a trainer information package in about six months, but not along the lines of my needs.

A friend tried notices on computer bulletin boards. It was a dead-end. Nothing.

It struck me. Information I sought, in the form I needed, did not exist, anywhere. Further, I was wasting a good thing, using it as only a personal betting tool. Continuing as I was should have brought me at least $100,000 a year; but a Trainers Database would be a one-of-a-kind item. And in the hands of professional marketing people, it might be worth millions! I liked the sound of that. I knew nothing about marketing, but had learned a great deal about gathering details on trainers. It seemed to be the only reasonable course.

I would set up a research facility, hire and train sufficient help to investigate every trainer operating at any racetrack with a *Daily Racing Form* Purse Value Index (PVI) of "10" or over. This would effectively cover all the major racing circuits in the country. I'd begin with the East Coast.

My choice of location for this facility was determined by two things.

The greed and hypocrisy of state governments trying to keep every dollar within the state available for taxation, continues to prohibit making a bet across the state line. However, I had a New York OTB telephone account and a direct line I could dial from anywhere in the country (station-to-station). My information on northern trainers was sufficient to make betting there worthwhile. It would also be worthwhile to have a Philadelphia Park Phonebet account (though this one proved some trouble to use and never really got off the ground). My Hialeah Tel-A-Bet account was still good and I was told they were planning to expand to Gulfstream the following season. (They didn't, but this was an influence at the time).

It seemed, geographically speaking, only one region of racing was outside my ability to bet; New Jersey and Maryland. Neither of these states offered OTB or telephone convenience. Any betting to be done in these states would have to be at the window. My decision was made for me. Anybody drawing a string from Laurel to Monmouth and bending it in the middle can see how I came up with Delaware.

As a licensed pilot, a rented plane could have me anywhere I needed to be in an hour. Newark, Delaware proved an excellent choice and, without the remotest suspicion of the disaster to come, I set up my company, Race-Search, Inc. in April.

The prospect of creating something that did not exist took my imagination. I only had about $18,000 at the time, but as soon as things were organized I'd begin betting again and take up whatever slack was needed. It was easy diving into the details of office space; furniture and equipment, hiring and training five people, setting out the road signs to where I expected to end up. It was new, and interesting. Every minute was enjoyable until I ran into a big, big problem.

Newark, Delaware was a great location in every respect but one. The *Daily Racing Form* did not cover Florida racing in the local editions. Florida was where I had the bulk of my best information. Betting Florida racing was to provide my income until I could fill in the other areas, and now, zip. I could get the *Form's* past performances on every bullring within 300 miles, but Florida was out; and I was only sixty-five miles south of the Hightstown presses.

First-class mail to a P.O. Box made it two out of seven tries. My pleas to their circulation department seemed to fall on deaf ears and it was frustrating, to say the least. This situation was causing me an awful lot of problems. It was incongruous to be able to win at the races, yet, keep tripping over newspaper delivery. Ridiculous! But, there I sat, too far in to get out.

Why should I have only one problem? Another, an expected one, came sooner than I anticipated. My help was too efficient. Information was being piled up so fast, all I could do to was keep track of the flow.  Very soon, even that limited control would vanish.  Computerizing could not be put off.  That, of course, brought it's own raft of new, unfamiliar problems.  My money was nearly gone.

What started as a search to learn how William Knuck scored with a "$69 Crimson Anvil" was proving to be a pit of quicksand, and I was up to my waste.

"Why don't you sell some of your information?" asked Jodi.  She was among the first I hired.  After putting in eight hours for me, she took the night shift, caring for the horses used by the Wilmington Police Department.  In her spare time she rode exercise at Delaware Park.  Very pretty and bright; a very down-home girl.  I liked her.  It seemed like a dumb question.

Maybe not so dumb.  I had to sell something!

My plan since that March was to create a one-of-a-kind database and sell it to some individual or firm with marketing expertise.  Selling the information short of that would compromise the integrity... but not if I sold only a little, to a limited number...

Out of this necessity, we put together a program that I thought would generate income without giving up too large a slice.  The plan (later called our Subscriber Program) was an offer to 100 people through seminars from Calder to Saratoga, the names of trainers who were showing successful and profitable patterns in that particular area.  The first "edition" of *Handicapping Trainers* was included with the offer.

Additionally, I agreed to examine the *Daily Racing Form* every day (all major tracks) to see if any races that day offered opportunities described in my guide.  If any were found, I agreed to put this information on a tape recording that subscribers could access by telephone every morning after 10 o'clock.  Examining forty races for trainers with a pattern takes only thirty minutes.  The bet is there, or it's not.  There's no ambivalence.

It took several seminars to get this package wrapped well enough to be of more than passing interest; even longer for our computers to catch up with the demand it created. Eventually, it smoothed out nicely, offering a considerable fringe benefit: validation. The morning tape recording named the day, track, race and trainer; effectively putting me (and my method) on the hook for all to see. An automatic $2 bet on every opportunity mentioned on this tape brought the precise results pictured on the regional graphs.

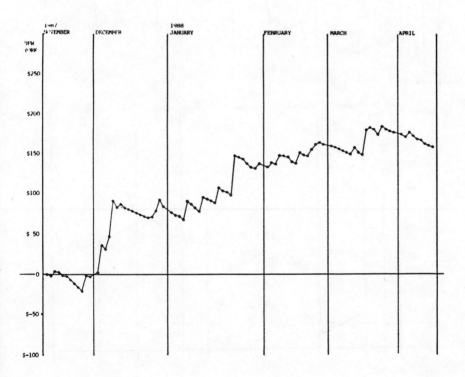

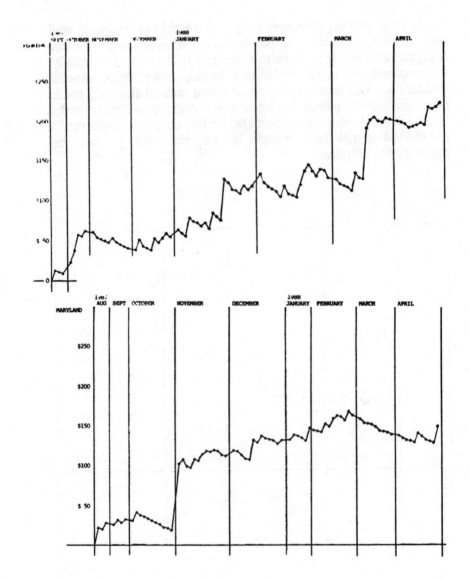

After two years, the results of this activity painted a brighter picture than the one imagined when Saint Cambridge came through for Neal Winick. The concept proved practical at every level; from following the single trainer with one discernable pattern, to the hundreds we eventually uncovered. It worked! It worked over and over.

Now the exiliration of Saint Cambridge and OK Fine was long gone. Doubt and wonder were gone, too. Handicapping trainers worked, but the excitement of pioneering had disolved. The principles, systems and database were all in place with more than sufficient validation. The package was very neatly wrapped, but Race-Search, Inc. taught me that running a company was not my calling in life. A ten day vacation to the Virgin Islands got me away long enough to step back and look. For my mental well-being, I decided to put it all on the shelf.

When will the effort to develop this database pay off to its fullest potential? Only time will tell. But one thing is certain -- more will be written about Race-Search, Inc.!

# CHAPTER TEN
# Discipline

# Discipline

The Subscriber Program described earlier has kept me in daily touch with many fine people who continue to enjoy the benefits. Unfortunately, many failed to realize the full potential of what was at hand. Those who attended the seminars were cautioned that this was not a way of picking winners of races. It was new, and made completely new demands on a bettor. All that could be presented was the opportunity. Their own application would determine the end.

The discipline required for the kind of venture described here is hard to manage for the average horseplayer, in whom the habit of "forcing action" is very strong. Handicapping trainers severely limits action. Tension (another term for excitement) is minimal because the outcome of any single race is unimportant. Of course, it's nice to win, now! But we're not betting on a horse or a race. A win, now, means x number of losses next week or next month. They are definitely there.

This new technique requires one to relax, and let the wins come in their own time. Not worrying about the tote board keeps the blood pressure down; and a smile on a sleeping face. This is not easy for any person craving the action of playing horses and may not even be welcome. That random "thrill" of winning becomes jaded as part of a foregone conclusion. It isn't for everyone. However, for the person who never saw a race, a student, or one in search of an annuity, investing in trainers has great potential.

If a horseplayer has not found a winning formula after three or four years, he's already learned dozens of ways to lose. Changing these ways will not be easy. So many conditions in this plan will turn his stomach; require him to go against many things he believes gospel. He will have to be an extraordinary person to bet into 90% of the "plays" that look terrible in their last races, show no workouts or recent conditioning, go up in class, at untried distances and surfaces or have never raced before. It's a lot to ask of a horseplayer.

He may dabble with this new thing but, for most, too much work is involved in the beginning. Losing isn't so bad as long as it's simple. The Railbird has practically no chance at all except with the high visibility situations. A college student on the other hand, has no bad habits to overcome.

Example: The student and the horseplayer each go at it with this plan. A "play" appearing in the entries must be made and there's no question to be asked or decision to be made. The "play'" must be bet.

The student will make it because that's what the plan dictates. The horseplayer will examine the rest of the field, the handicappers selections; creating conflict. "Tudor Jours" on August 29 was the worst looking animal in the race, except for one possible exception. The student wouldn't realize this, the horseplayer would.

# CHAPTER ELEVEN
# Investing in the Trainer

# Investing in the Trainer

Pari-mutuel windows have been called, the poor man's stock market, and the comparison is well made. Most significant among the differences is a fact, the stock market is given to long term investing and one seldom, if ever, hears anything about long term investing at the track.

There are Martingales and progression systems applied here and there, but few, if any, work consistently or don't involve very high risk along the line. It's accepted, the mutual windows offer only short term speculation; in and out in 1:11 and 4. You win or lose. The next race is a whole new prize.

Investing in trainers changes this picture. One no longer is betting on a horse, but "investing" in the trainer's already proven ability to succeed under certain, definite conditions. He may not do it in today's race but that part has lost its importance. What is important now is that the investor get his money down whenever this trainer enters a horse under his winning Index.

Just as there are blue chip stocks, there are blue chip trainers, many yet unknown to the public. Research has proven this and one such blue chip trainer was examined earlier, Frank A. Alexander, who has enjoyed success in Maryland, Florida, and lately up and down the east coast. When the *Racing Form* shows he has a runner going, he gets a lot of respect in the betting and over all, he does pretty well. He doesn't get the writeups of Lukas, Stephens, Wittingham, et.al., but when it comes to getting a "particular" job done, not one of the above is better.

About this particular job. My report on Frank Alexander in October:

"A poor bet with FTS and FTS2. Will occasionally win but it's a long time in between. Less than half are in the money. (Still, they show a 90% profit.) Poor bet with a 1 1/2 month Layoff, or ANY Layoff coming back to 6 furlongs. Very strong (blue chip) with slightly longer Lay-offs; 2-3.5 months coming back to 7 furlongs or the Turf. In these he is winning 6 of 12 at odds of 13, 10, 9, 7, 7, and 6 to 1 (427%). Very strong (blue chip) with anything he puts on the Turf for the first time. (3 for 4 returning 200% net profit. The one that failed to win finished 7th by only 1 length."

These performance values held close the rest of the year. The poorest of his profitable Index, FTS and FTS2, showed 84% net for 1986 and smothered anything Smith-Barney or Merrill Lynch were selling, and this, again, was the shallowest area of his expertise. (No offense intended the brokers but, showing only 84%, a trainer doesn't even get on the list. 150% is the minimum unless the trainer shows a great deal of activity, in which case we'll accept 100%. Many show over 500% net). Frank was deadly with horses he put on the turf for the first time. With certain Layoffs he demonstrates genius.

Consider the similarities between an investment in a stock, and an investment in Frank Alexander. In the end, that is what all this is about: investing.

Before investing in a company, the broker will research its history and that of its management. Before investing in Frank Alexander we research *his* history of performance in all the situations outside the normal routine of racing. We want to know in what situations (if any) he demonstrates superior performance and management skill.

The broker, examining the company, learns the top selling product is generating over 400% before overhead; which, of course, chews much of this figure away with plant overhead, payroll, pension plans, insurance and everything having any effect on the monetary structure. Melting it down, the broker sees profit on the bottom line. It appears a good buy and could (almost) guarantee a holder 22%. But with stocks, you have to buy the whole package, including one promising product.

An investment in Frank Alexander, however, presents an incredibly unique opportunity, unheard of in the conventional market; the opportunity to buy directly into Frank Alexander's best products without one penny going to overhead. (I've run this by many in the conventional business world and, almost without exception, they get that "glassy" look Columbus saw so much of during 7 years on his knees at Isabella's court. It's a little outside their cage).

Frank has his overhead; stable costs, employees, vet bills, feed bills, but so what? We don't have to invest in any of that. He also has some poor running horses in his barn but we don't bet on them; they're part of Frank Alexander's overhead, not ours. Frank is the company and horses are only the medium for marketing his products (Index), good and bad. We only buy into Frank's good products. We only buy into his layoff runners (under certain conditions) and his entries on the turf for the first time (L2-3 and FTT). On everything else, we pass. We skim the cream off the top. Forget Frank's stakes horses, his 2nd and 3rd time starters, his four month layoffs, shippers and fastbacks. We can invest only in Frank Alexander's best products. We don't have the same luxury investing in a company. In the conventional investment community, this is unheard of.

It was noted earlier that in making the investment in Frank Alexander, nothing needs to be decided. We don't have to think. We need only read, and do. Every time Frank Alexander runs a horse on the turf for the first time, we get our $2 down; every time. We never have to look at the rest of the field or the professional's selections; the Bute and Lasix lists; the jockey stats, mud caulks, nothing. We do nothing except get our $2 in. No decisions. Frank has already done all of that for us before he entered his horse in the race. We don't listen to our instincts or to the owner of the horse. We don't even listen to Frank Alexander because he's already told us everything we need to know. We need only get our $2 down and relax.

Frank's entry may not win todays race. We may not recover our investment immediately; then, neither does the man investing in building a house. The dozer that clears the site has to be paid when he's done his job, as part of the builder's investment.

Frank's entry doesn't have to win today. All Frank has to do is run another FTT; and another and another. We're not betting on a "horse race." We are investing in a highly skilled professional's proven ability to succeed under certain and particular conditions. We invest in the cream of Frank Alexander & Company, and not five cents in the overhead.

Insider trading; and it's legal. 22% may be great on Wall Street, but a handicapper of trainers who cannot do substantially better is probably "gambling" somewhere along the line.

# CHAPTER TWELVE
# Money Management

# Money Management

Before a money management plan can be decided, one's objective must be defined from a choice of two: horseplaying and investing.

Generally, the horseplayer wants "action;" six or seven bets a day that have some degree of probability. The most positive aspects of handicapping trainers won't satisfy that need. *Three or four good bets a week is typical activity with this approach* (assuming the betting is confined to one track). However, negative information becomes a part of every race and every decision-making process by eliminating horses that have proven dead in this situation. If the "dead" horse happens to be a favorite, great possibilities are opened for any of the exotic wagers. Knowing what *not* to do is valuable to *any* degree of activity.

The investor, on the other hand, has no use for negative information at all. It is the small investor (speculator) who can squeeze the most out of handicapping trainers; the person who enjoys watching the ticker at the brokerage, ready to pounce on whatever opportunity is presented. He doesn't need "action" every 25 minutes. The trading opportunities for this person are roughly equivalent to the appearance of "positive" opportunities handicapping trainers will offer at the track. He may not be able to invest as much as he'd like on each opportunity (without damaging the odds) but he won't have to. The percentage of profit in handicapping trainers is calculated in numbers conventional investors see only in their daydreams, 100%-1000%.

There is no reason why the horseplayer can not take full advantage of both the positive *and* negative if he can find the time to handicap the horses *and* keep his trainer records up to date.  To enjoy the full benefits of handicapping trainers, both investor and horseplayer must approach it as an investment plan; no speculating or guesswork is involved.  Decisions to be made will be very few.  For those who use handicapping trainers only as "spot play," the benefits will still be evident, but less certain. For those who are more serious, the route is in plain view; it's simply a matter of going.

It was mentioned earlier, the major destroyer of most plans is a lack of discipline.  If we use the investment approach, a shortage of ready coin is also a critical factor.  Assuming discipline, we approach the other.  The formula presented should allow the investor nearly all the security attached to a passbook account.

A minimum operation begins with the discovery of ONE TRAINER who has ONE INDEX that he succeeds with on a consistent basis. The record printed below is real, and provides enough information to allow certain conclusions after we learn the numbers.  Looking at John Lenzini Jr.'s record, we want to know what to expect if we invest in his "Cl-1" Index (betting his horse in the first race after the claim, regardless of any conditions that are present).

Lenzini, John J. Jr.    RECORD WITH CLAIMED HORSES FOR NEXT 3 RACES    PAGE 1

| CLAIM DATE | HORSE NAME | CLAIM RACE | CLAIM TRACK | CLAIM PRICE | FIN | NEW OWNER | INTERVAL #1 | CLASS OF 1st RACE | FIN #1 | ODDS | FIN #2 | ODDS | FIN #3 | ODDS |
|---|---|---|---|---|---|---|---|---|---|---|---|---|---|---|
| 05/30/86 | Karabar | 2 | BEL | 14000 | 6 | Amendola | 20 | ALW | 1 | 12 | | | 0 | 0 |
| 09/11/86 | Flying Skipper | 2 | BEL | 25000 | 3 | Amendola | 15 | 35000 | 1 | 3 | 0 | 0 | 0 | 0 |
| 09/17/86 | Capo Cane | 2 | BEL | 25000 | 1 | Amendola | 22 | 35000 | 6 | 1 | 1 | 2 | 2 | 6 |
| 10/13/86 | Military Reaction | 1 | WO | 32000 | 1 | Amendola | 114 | NW1 | 10 | 3 | 5 | 2 | 4 | 7 |
| 10/24/86 | Zango | 9 | AQU | 17500 | 12 | Amendola | 1 | | 2 | 2 | 7 | 2 | 4 | 2 |
| 10/24/86 | Karabar | 4 | AQU | 22500 | 2 | Amendola | 30 | 30000 | 7 | 4 | 7 | 2 | 2 | 1 |
| 10/25/86 | Cross Your Feather | 4 | WO | 20000 | 2 | Cedar Valle | 114 | 25000 | 1 | 6 | 2 | 2 | 1 | 3 |
| 11/22/86 | Just Gorgeous | 1 | AQU | 35000 | 7 | Gold-N-Oats | 15 | 45000 | 2 | 3 | 2 | 2 | 2 | 2 |
| 11/23/86 | Big Jim Taylor | 1 | AQU | 20000 | 7 | Amendola | 13 | 25000 | 2 | 4 | 2 | 2 | 1 | 3 |
| 11/24/86 | Lead The Way | 1 | AQU | 17500 | 2 | Gold-N-Oats | 8 | 22500 | 1 | 9 | 1 | 1 | 3 | 3 |
| 12/04/86 | Gigaletree | 4 | AQU | 47000 | 2 | Gold-N-Oats | 16 | NW1 | 2 | 4 | 2 | 1 | 3 | 7 |
| 12/13/86 | Onnagata | 9 | AQU | 25000 | 9 | Gold-N-Oats | 14 | 35000 | 6 | 9 | 3 | 2 | 2 | 2 |
| 12/26/86 | Gold Crop | 9 | AQU | 175000 | 1 | Gold-N-Oats | 20 | 25000 | 3 | 3 | 4 | 3 | 1 | 2 |
| 01/08/87 | Social Gesture | 9 | AQU | 14000 | 2 | Cedar Valle | 21 | 17500 | 2 | 2 | 4 | 2 | 4 | 4 |
| 01/29/87 | Greensboro | 5 | AQU | 35000 | 8 | Gold-N-Oats | 23 | NW1 | 2 | 2 | 3 | 6 | 4 | 4 |
| 01/30/87 | Summer Tale | 9 | AQU | 35000 | 3 | Gold-N-Oats | 21 | NW3 | 1 | 10 | 1 | 3 | 2 | 2 |
| 01/31/87 | Private Iron | 2 | AQU | 22500 | 2 | Cedar Valle | 14 | 32500 | 8 | 5 | 3 | 3 | 1 | 2 |
| 02/14/87 | Following Star | 1 | AQU | 32500 | 1 | Cedar Valle | 46 | 14000 | 3 | 1 | 3 | 3 | 6 | 2 |
| 02/15/87 | Arctic Song | 2 | AQU | 35000 | 2 | Cedar Valle | 10 | 45000 | 3 | 2 | 3 | 1 | 6 | 2 |
| 03/22/87 | AmongtheChosenFew | 9 | AQU | 14000 | 2 | Cedar Valle | 14 | 17500 | 6 | 3 | 7 | 2 | 6 | 4 |
| 03/29/87 | Private Iron | 5 | AQU | 25000 | 2 | Cedar Valle | 24 | 35000 | 5 | 2 | 1 | 6 | 5 | 1 |
| 04/06/87 | Biomostar | 3 | AQU | 30000 | 1 | Cedar Valle | 19 | 50000 | 3 | 2 | 2 | 5 | 5 | 4 |
| 07/27/87 | Getreadyfortheshow | 3 | BEL | 100000 | 1 | Cedar Valle | 14 | ALW | 4 | 19 | 7 | 4 | 5 | 4 |
| 08/09/87 | Dustititous | 9 | SAR | 20000 | 11 | Cedar Valle | 10 | 25000 | 12 | 12 | 4 | 5 | 1 | 1 |
| 10/28/87 | Scottish Monk | 1 | AQU | 35000 | 8 | Cedar Valle | 18 | 50000 | 5 | 11 | 8 | 30 | 1 | 17 |
| 12/19/87 | Peppy Le Pew | 2 | AQU | 35000 | 2 | Cedar Valle | 9 | 45000 | 1 | 4 | 0 | 0 | 0 | 0 |
| 12/31/87 | Caserell | 9 | AQU | 25000 | 21 | Cedar Valle | 32 | 17500 | 1 | 3 | 0 | 0 | 0 | 0 |
| 01/27/88 | Leraontov | 5 | AQU | 50000 | 4 | Cedar Valle | 25 | ALW | 4 | 13 | 1 | 25 | 0 | 0 |
| 01/28/88 | Dancing Socks | 1 | AQU | 15500 | 4 | Cedar Valle | 22 | 35000 | 6 | 6 | 2 | 4 | 0 | 0 |
| 02/03/88 | Pawn The Silver | 4 | AQU | 30000 | 7 | Cedar Valle | 17 | 50000 | 7 | 6 | 2 | 13 | 1 | 3 |
| 02/19/88 | My Funny Face | 2 | AQU | 25000 | 7 | Cedar Valle | 10 | ALW | 3 | 1 | 8 | 6 | 4 | 2 |
| 02/21/88 | Peppy Le Pew | 5 | AQU | 35000 | 3 | Cedar Valle | 12 | 50000 | 1 | 17 | 0 | 0 | 0 | 0 |

How many times did he run this Index?   32

How many times did he win with it?   8

We have to plan ahead for his next 32 races in this Index. Winning one out of four (losing nine in a row at one point), it will not be unreasonable for him to lose ten or twelve in a row, before scoring again.   Even then, we have no guarantee the payoff will recover our total previous investment.   We will probably get it back in bits and pieces, however, we must continue to cover him for this program to work.

Murphy is watching what you're doing, and he begins to grin. He doesn't have any control over your chosen trainer's expertise, but he can see to it that everybody gets stretched to the breaking point; and he will.

Your trainer will win at least six times with the next thirty two Index Runners, but Murphy will see to it those wins come on race numbers 27 through 32.   Count on it.

Before you can begin to invest in this trainer you must have a minimum of $52. and be prepared to *invest it all without hesitation*.   There is no other choice, if you want to keep it safe. If you want to gamble, begin with $20 or $30: KNOW that your risk is much greater than afforded a passbook account. You can not afford to run out of capital.   The odds are very good your man will come through much earlier; the 6th, 7th or 8th race, but you can not count on it.   You must not; if you want to make a safe investment.

Want to operate at a $20 level?   You need $520 before making your first investment.   $100 level?   You need $2,600. and remember, we're talking about ONE trainer with ONE Index. For each additional Trainer/Index you want to take on, you need that same amount in addition.

A pictorial understanding of this process is achieved if you imagine that each single Trainer/Index is a slowly turning wheel. The above trainer's wheel would be divided in thirty two pie-slice sections representing his 32-race history. Spaced evenly around the outside of this wheel are eight large red dots, representing the eight wins in his history. The spacing of the red dots is a theoretical anticipation; three losses, then a win; three more losses, then a win. They won't come that way. They didn't in his history, either. This wheel is only a representation of our expectations.

When you take this Trainer/Index on, you must imagine his eight wins (you will settle for six) somewhere on that wheel, but you don't know where. Each time an Index runner loses, the wheel turns one notch closer to the next win, somewhere in that cycle.

It is important and gratifying to know that each of these wheels, one trainer with one Index, is a completely independent operation. It is not related to any other wheel in any way; even if you are running a single trainer with two or three Indexes. No single Index has any relationship to any other. Each one is a single wheel, turning in its own time and space.

If a wheel should grind to a halt; (the trainer tails off in the Index) this fact can have no influence on any other wheel in your operation. There can never be any domino effect caused by a one trainer failing to live up to expectations.

Wheels *will* grind to a halt, but very seldom. If enough care and discrimination is part of your original selection process, these skilled professionals go on and on. The rate you will uncover a *new* trainer with an Index is far more rapid than the cancellation rate. In more than two years, fewer than two dozen were cancelled and four were seriously regretted. On the day a decision to cancel was made, three of them scored over 15-to-1; the other came through two races later. Lenzini is one that was canned for not having enough in the kitty. I mentioned this news on the morning tape recording and that afternoon he won with "Peppy LePew" paying $36. It happens.

Presently, there are over 300 individual Trainer/Index available to me in the East. They turn slowly, but merrily.

Another optional part of money management involves a sliding scale of Trainer/Index available to you. If there are only a few, you can afford to operate at a higher unit (bet) level. As the number of Trainer/Index increases, you can, if you choose, reduce your unit level on each, instead of going into your pocket for more capital. Then, as profits are added to the operating bank, the unit level can be stepped back up.

### Off-Track and Telephone Betting

The proliferation of Off-Track Betting facilities (electronic, telephone, etc.) suggests a day, not far off, when we can sit in our living room and bet a horse anywhere in the country, by telephone or a computer terminal like the ones presently in use at some tracks. Having trainer information at outlying tracks is certainly a good thing, but most OTB operations at this time present a trade-off in advantages, particularly to the horseplayer (as distinguished from the investor).

On one hand, you have little or no chance to examine the odds that may indicate one of the exotic bets has greater potential than a straight win, or visa-versa. On the other, you are spared much of the pre-race anxiety brought on by tote-board fluctuations, the gossip of the "smart money" seated all around you, and actually seeing your selection foaming and frothing in the post parade.

Most OTB parlors show odds on TV monitors but their attention to pre-race changes often wanders, hindering the decision process. This is no time to suffer that uncertainty because handicapping trainers brings a potential to exotics that can't be realized in other ways.

For exotic purposes, almost every race quadruples in value because your "key" horse has been (nearly always) carefully hidden from the public. You're starting out with a price. Odds favor one of the others being a price also (two-thirds of the time). The potential for a great payoff is far better than any keyed to a favorite.

This complaint regarding OTB attention to details will diminish in volume as current technology improves.

**Additional Note**

"I lost 25 bets in a row, and you tell me there's no problem?!"

The transition from betting horses to investing in trainers is not an easy one, evidenced by a New York subscriber who, after losing his first six bets in a row, began calling daily, much concerned he was not getting his money's worth. The fact that under this program, one is not betting horses or races, but INVESTING in proven trainers is not easy on which to get a grip.

Consider: One Trainer with one Index showing a history of 200% profit. We do not know when he will strike again, we only know he will. He may lose 5, 6, 7 in a row, then hit with an 11 to 1 shot and there we are with a good profit on our investment. Now, we settle back and wait two, three, or four months for him to do it again. He will. We only have to be there when he does.

Now, instead of waiting four months to cash our next ticket, let's take on another trainer doing the same thing and hopefully we only have to wait two months between cashings. You have two Trainer/Index that are reasonably expected to lose five or six races before scoring again (this keeps the public off their backs). If both trainers lose their five bets around the same time, you're down ten in a row with only two trainers. Still, nothing is wrong. Each will do his thing, as you expect, but meanwhile, you're down ten in a row.

Carrying more than 15 Trainer/Index, it should be easy to understand how this situation can appear to get out of hand when in fact, it is not. It's possible. It's a good idea to keep the initial betting level small until the program builds it's own bank, whereupon small increases from time to time will keep the risk factor out in the street. This is an investment plan and one has to be prepared to *make* an investment. It can't be done on "short money" any easier than horseplaying.

The second hardest thing to accept is laying good money on some of the 40 to 1 shots that come up. "No way," you say. There's nothing to be done about this until one of those 40 to 1 shots you chose to "pass" comes home in front. It's the only way the lesson is learned. When the trainer is there, get beside him.

# CHAPTER THIRTEEN
# Computers

# Computers

It's impossible to overstate the necessity of a personal computer. Today, they are inexpensive and easy to use. Everyone should own one or, at the very least, know how to use one. By following even one track, there comes a time these files can no longer be managed by hand; it's too much. Things go well for seven or eight months; then you notice a pinch; a shortage of time; unfinished searches. The message is clear. You fall hopelessly behind, shortchanging your potential, or get a computer.

Beginning by hand, as I did, another problem surfaces immediately. You have this ton of handwritten data that now has to be loaded into the new computer (duplicating much of your previous effort).

Having a PC at the outset will cancel the above problem and also cut out two very tedious steps in collecting; the alphabetical handwritten pages and the individual trainer's record (typewritten). This data is now taken from the *Racing Form* after coding, then entered directly on a computer screen designed to accept whatever information you are collecting. When complete, each screen becomes the permanent record of one Index runner and is logged under the trainer's name. These files reside permanently on the hard disk.

The card file of claims is also eliminated. This information is entered on a screen set up to log all details of the claim and follow the claimed horse through the next three races. This, too, is indexed on trainer but resides in a different file on the hard disk.

When my own need arose, I knew only how to spell the word, but was lucky enough to find a programmer who could understand the needs as they were described to him. He knew nothing about racing. Together we created the first working program to accommodate all of the parameters described in this book, and many not even mentioned. It didn't take long to outgrow the first 40 megabytes.

The following is a September, 1987 search through Maryland racing that explains much of the capability. It is a simple and logical procedure that searches tens of thousands of records in only minutes; performing a task that would take at least a week for a hand operation.

This information, a computer Question and Answer exercise, was prepared to illustrate a point; to show the procedure and electronics involved in finding a precise answer. The data from which this exercise was prepared is not complete; but was abbreviated because of space limitations. The result, however, is a discovered fact. The trainer uncovered by this search continued to perform exactly as this exercise predicted.

At the beginning, we have no idea "who's who" in Maryland, but all of the data we need to learn has been meticulously entered in the computer at considerable expense.

Choosing one of the many Index situations we track, (L1-3), we will ask if any trainers show a profitable skill in this situation (bringing horses back from a Layoff of 1.5 to 3.5 months). Forty days is the minimum time we record as a Layoff; calling it "L1-3" instead of "L1.5-3.5" makes it easier on the computer. It knows what to look for.

Instead of using a "batch command," (a complex command that will perform every stage in sequence, with a single keystroke), we proceed one step at a time. First, we need to know who all the winners were so we begin by sifting away all the chaff.

NOTE: You've seen the label, "Computer Generated..." This means, some results are "estimated" using contiguous data; values are placed where there are no facts to support them.

We "generate" nothing. We only want what the computer knows; not what it "indicates, projects, or regards as probable." When we have a result from the facts, if there is any "generating" to be done, we'll do it ourselves.

"LIST ALL 1st AND 2nd PLACE FINISHERS, INDEX L1-3, AT PIMLICO OR LAUREL IN 1986 AND 1987." (Following is an abbreviated list of an actual search made early in August, 1987. Exact copies of this search were given out at a number of seminars in September and October of that year.)

| DATE | RACE | TRK | DIST | INDEX 1 & 2 | HORSE NAME | AGE | CLASS | FIN | ODDS | TRAINER |
|------|------|-----|------|-------------|------------|-----|-------|-----|------|---------|
| 03/02/86 | 3 | LRL | 6.5 | L1.5 | DUELING DAL | 3 | X6 | 1 | 12.0 | Mayo, Larry |
| 03/02/87 | 5 | LRL | 6.5 | L1.5 | FIVE STAR P | 3 | X6 | 2 | 2.3 | Hendricks, Frank |
| 03/02/87 | 8 | LRL | 6.5 | L2.5 | E. A. BISHO | 3 | C25 | 2 | 8.0 | Alfano, Ronald A. |
| 03/10/87 | 8 | LRL | 6 | L2 | BAL DU BOIS | 3 | NW2 | 1 | 19.2 | Hadry, Charles H. |
| 03/13/87 | 5 | LRL | 6 | L2 | ROCK PLAYER | 3 | X30 | 2 | 29.2 | Kern, Berkley W. |
| 03/13/87 | 7 | LRL | 6 | L1.5 | PLAYING POL | 4 | NW2 | 1 | 3.3 | Tammaro, John III |
| 03/13/87 | 8 | LRL | 8.5 | L2 | CHIC WEED | 4 | C14 | 1 | 2.5 | Leatherbury, King |
| 03/13/87 | 9 | LRL | 6.5 | L2 | FOOT STONE | 4 | NW3 | 1 | 2.4 | Clark, Henry S. |
| 03/17/86 | 5 | LRL | 6 | L3 | HARFORD HIL | 3 | MSW | 2 | 5.8 | Testerman, Valora |
| 03/17/86 | 9 | LRL | 6.5 | L2.5 | DOVER RIDGE | 4 | C50 | 1 | 1.4 | Hadry, Charles H. |
| 03/21/87 | 3 | LRL | 7 | L1.5 | GRAND CASCA | 4 | C5 | 1 | 14.7 | Kline, James W. |
| 03/21/87 | 10 | LRL | 6.5 | L1.5 | BLUE AND BO | 3 | X6 | 1 | 3.6 | Simpson, James P. |
| 03/23/87 | 8 | PIM | 6 | L2 | BEAR FEET | 4 | NW3 | 1 | 3.3 | Tagg, Barclay |
| 03/24/87 | 5 | PIM | 8.5 | L1.5 | MISS JESSIC | 4 | CT | 1 | 5.6 | Green, Martha C. |
| 03/24/87 | 7 | PIM | 6 | L1.5 | DARK CHALLE | 4 | C14 | 1 | 5.5 | Horning, Lawrence |
| 03/24/87 | 10 | PIM | 8.5 | L1.5 | HOGAN'S LAD | 3 | X6 | 1 | 9.6 | Peacock, Roy M. |
| 03/24/87 | 10 | PIM | 8.5 | L1.5 | SECOND MARP | 3 | X6 | 2 | 4.5 | Allen, Harold A. |

| DATE | RACE | TRK | DIST | INDEX 1 & 2 | | HORSE NAME | AGE | CLASS | FIN | ODDS | TRAINER |
|------|------|-----|------|-------------|--|------------|-----|-------|-----|------|---------|
| 03/27/86 | 5 | PIM | 6 | L2 | | MARDI GRAS | 4 | C5 | 1 | 4.8 | Pruce, Ellis Y. |
| 03/27/86 | 7 | PIM | 8.5 | L1.5 | | PRINCELY BU | 3 | X16 | 1 | 35.2 | Pearce, Ross R. |
| 03/27/86 | 9 | PIM | 9 | L1.5 | | SCOTCH HEAT | 4 | NW$ | 1 | 5.6 | Mobberley, John C |
| 03/30/87 | 3 | PIM | 6 | L3.5 | | SILVER CHAR | 3 | X11 | 2 | 39.2 | Ayres, Joseph W. |
| 03/31/87 | 5 | PIM | 6 | L3 | | SHORT ENCOU | 3 | X6 | 2 | 2.7 | Heil, Nancy B. |
| 03/31/87 | 8 | PIM | 6 | L2.5 | | TITAN RIBOT | 4 | C25 | 1 | .9 | Wiggins, Deborah |
| 04/03/87 | 4 | PIM | 6 | L2.5 | | THESPIS | 3 | C30 | 2 | 5.9 | Simpson, James P. |
| 03/03/87 | 8 | PIM | 6 | L2 | | EARNING POW | 4 | C8 | 1 | 6.4 | Kidwell, Robert W |
| 04/04/87 | 7 | PIM | 6 | L2.5 | | GET THE HOO | 3 | MSW | 2 | 5.4 | Goswell, Michael |
| 04/06/87 | 1 | PIM | 6 | L1.5 | | TARGET SHIP | 4 | C6 | 2 | 4.1 | Stancer, Sandra |
| 04/06/87 | 5 | PIM | 9 | L3 | | EDGAR'S GIR | 4 | C5 | 1 | 1.5 | Leatherbury, King |
| 04/11/87 | 9 | PIM | 6 | L3 | | SUDDEN FLAR | 3 | STK | 2 | 5.5 | Miller, Jane |
| 05/05/87 | 3 | PIM | 6 | L1.5 | | ATTITUDE AD | 3 | X6 | 1 | 2.2 | Tammaro, John III |
| 05/09/87 | 3 | PIM | 6 | L1.5 | | HASTY CANNO | 4 | C5 | 1 | 5.6 | Johnson, Norman A |
| 05/09/87 | 10 | PIM | 8.5T | L1.5 | | COVERT OPER | 4 | C50 | 1 | 4.3 | Potts, Dennis |
| 05/13/87 | 3 | PIM | 9 | L1.5 | | JAN'S MAN | 3 | X6 | 2 | 12.3 | Briones, Pedro |
| 05/14/87 | 7 | PIM | 6 | L1.5 | | SHEBEEN | 3 | C6 | 2 | 7.3 | Murphy, James W. |
| 05/18/87 | 5 | PIM | 6 | L1.5 | | FEISTY | 4 | C5 | 2 | 47.7 | Maffay, Robert L. |
| 05/18/87 | 10 | PIM | 6 | L1.5 | | GINGER SNAP | 3 | C11 | 1 | 4.3 | Mitchell, Thomas |
| 05/20/87 | 3 | PIM | 6 | L2 | | GEORGIA'S E | 3 | X6 | 1 | 2.8 | Lewis, Charles R. |
| 05/20/87 | 8 | PIM | 6 | L1.5 | | MUSCOVY DUC | 3 | NW2 | 1 | 3.3 | Caviness, Thomas |
| 05/21/87 | 1 | PIM | 6 | L1.5 | | LAKE TOBA | 3 | X30 | 1 | 4.3 | Christenson, Ralp |
| 05/21/87 | 3 | PIM | 6 | L3 | | UNPLAYABLE | 3 | X6 | 1 | 13.5 | Kosonavich, Georg |
| 05/21/87 | 7 | PIM | 6 | L2 | | APRIL RECIT | 3 | C11 | 1 | 7.5 | Pino, Michael V. |
| 05/21/87 | 8 | PIM | 6 | L1.5 | | NORLAND NAN | 3 | NW2 | 2 | 5.6 | Hadry, Charles H. |
| 05/23/87 | 2 | PIM | 9 | L1.5 | | IMACRUISEIN | 3 | X6 | 2 | 4.4 | Delp. Richard W. |
| 01/01/87 | 1 | LRL | 6.5 | L1.5 | | BANNER YET | 5 | C8 | 1 | 7.0 | Mobberley, John C |
| 01/02/87 | 3 | LRL | 6 | L2 | | AFTER THE F | 4 | X9 | 2 | 4.5 | Metz, Lawrence C. |
| 01/02/87 | 5 | LRL | 8 | L2.5 | | TAKE THE VO | 6 | C5 | 1 | 10.9 | Owens, Josephine |
| 01/02/87 | 10 | LRL | 7 | L2 | 2TS | COUNT DIXIE | 4 | X6 | 2 | 19.8 | Sipe, David L. |
| 05/30/87 | 1 | LRL | 6.5 | L2 | | CAPULET'S R | 3 | C5 | 2 | 1.8 | Mitchell, H. Stew |
| 06/01/87 | 6 | LRL | 8 | L1.5 | | SPOUSE EQUI | 3 | C11 | 1 | 2.9 | Campbell, Michael |
| 06/01/87 | 9 | LRL | 8.5 | L1.5 | | JUSAVIK | 4 | C25 | 2 | 1.1 | Hadry, Charles H. |
| 06/02/87 | 7 | LRL | 6T | L2 | FTT | BUSTER BANK | 3 | NW1 | 2 | 17.2 | Richardson, Grego |
| 06/04/87 | 5 | LRL | 6.5 | L1.5 | | UNLESS | 4 | C5 | 1 | 4.2 | Wolfendale, Howar |
| 06/04/87 | 9 | LRL | 7 | L2 | | ICE DEVISE | 3 | NW1 | 1 | 3.9 | Cartwright, Ronal |
| 06/07/87 | 5 | LRL | 6.5 | L1.5 | | AQUABAT | 3 | X6 | 1 | 12.1 | Small, Douglas R. |
| 06/08/87 | 7 | LRL | 8.5T | L1.7 | S | STAGE SIGN | 3 | C25 | 2 | 3.7 | Hicks, John W. II |
| 06/08/87 | 8 | LRL | 8.5T | L2.5 | S | CHRISTIANA | 3 | NW2 | 1 | 5.0 | Murphy, James W. |
| 06/14/87 | 3 | LRL | 6 | L2 | | CRAFTY RABB | 4 | NW2 | 1 | 6.1 | Ferris, Jerald M. |
| 06/15/87 | 1 | LRL | 6.5 | L2 | 2TS | KID FROM SK | 3 | X30 | 1 | 16.5 | Weiss, Richard |
| 06/15/87 | 8 | LRL | 6 | L2.5 | | WAINEE CHUR | 3 | NW3 | 1 | 1.9 | Peoples, Charles |
| 06/16/87 | 5 | LRL | 6 | L2 | | RARELY DOUB | 3 | X6 | 2 | 4.5 | Price, Angela |
| 06/22/87 | 4 | LRL | 6 | L1.7 | | BALSA WOOD | 4 | C8 | 1 | 1.0 | Kirk, Jeffrey C. |
| 06/22/87 | 6 | LRL | 8 | L1.7 | | GENERAL MOY | 3 | MSW | 1 | .7 | Garcia, Carlos A. |
| 01/03/87 | 4 | LRL | 7 | L1.5 | | EIGHTH EDIT | 5 | C11 | 2 | 2.3 | Dinatale, John F. |
| 01/03/87 | 10 | LRL | 6 | L2.5 | | MISS PORE | 5 | C5 | 2 | 15.9 | Vogelman, Raymond |
| 01/05/87 | 9 | LRL | 6 | L2 | | PAUL'S CATH | 4 | NW2 | 2 | 4.8 | Garcia, Carlos A. |
| 11/04/86 | 10 | LRL | 6 | L1.5 | | ROCKAID | 2 | X11 | 1 | 10.4 | Nixon, Richard |
| 11/07/86 | 5 | LRL | 6.5 | L3 | | KALLISTRE | 4 | C5 | 2 | 55.2 | Fraley, James E. |
| 11/11/86 | 6 | LRL | 6.5 | L1.5 | | BANNER YET | 3 | C6 | 1 | 8.7 | Mobberley, John C |

| DATE | RACE | TRK | DIST | INDEX 1 & 2 | HORSE NAME | AGE | CLASS | FIN | ODDS | TRAINER |
|---|---|---|---|---|---|---|---|---|---|---|
| 11/11/86 | 10 | LRL | 6 | L2 | COPPA HABIT | 2 | X8 | 1 | 9.7 | Aguirre, Horatio |
| 11/16/86 | 3 | LRL | 6 | L2.5 | OUR GIRL SU | 2 | X8 | 2 | 6.5 | Delp, Richard W. |
| 11/18/86 | 2 | LRL | 6 | L1.5 | DAMAVAND | 2 | X8 | 1 | 5.9 | Buntrock, Grant B |
| 10/03/86 | 7 | LRL | 8.5T | L1.5 | DARBRIELLE | 4 | NW$ | 2 | 1.7 | Murphy, James W. |
| 10/06/86 | 2 | LRL | 6 | L2 | PASS THE GR | 3 | MSW | 1 | 3.5 | Hicks, John W. II |
| 10/06/86 | 3 | LRL | 8 | L3.5 | THE GRAY PR | 3 | C5 | 2 | 6.3 | Schwartz, Ben |
| 10/07/86 | 7 | LRL | 6 | L1.5 | KAY'S LUCK | 3 | C14 | 2 | 1.4 | Caviness, Thomas |
| 10/09/86 | 7 | LRL | 8.5T | L2 FTT | WHERE'S BOB | 3 | NW3 | 1 | 2.0 | Jerkens, H. Allen |
| 01/11/87 | 3 | LRL | 6.5 | L3 | PRO BLUF | 3 | X11 | 1 | 4.8 | Garcia, Carlos A. |
| 11/23/86 | 8 | LRL | 6 | L2 | ONCE BITTEN | 3 | NW2 | 2 | 5.3 | Wilson, Gregory L |
| 11/25/86 | 6 | LRL | 6 | L3 | MS. STARLIG | 2 | X30 | 1 | 4.2 | Nichols, Lou |
| 12/29/66 | 3 | LRL | 6 | L1.5 | FORTY LOVE | 3 | C5 | 2 | 1.1 | Sipe, David L. |
| 12/29/86 | 4 | LRL | 8 | L2.5 | HEUBETCHACA | 3 | C8 | 2 | 3.0 | Leatherbury, King |
| 11/30/86 | 9 | LRL | 6 | L2 S | DEBTOR'S PR | 3 | HCP | 1 | 31.4 | Nanez, R. Carlos |
| 11/30/86 | 9 | LRL | 6 | L1.5 | NIGHT ABOVE | 3 | HCP | 2 | 2.1 | Van Berg, Jack C. |
| 07/02/87 | 1 | PIM | 6 | L1.5 | RELATION SH | 3 | C6 | 2 | 12.4 | Berry, William S. |
| 07/02/87 | 2 | PIM | 8.5 | L1.5 S | BEAU NASH | 3 | MSW | 2 | 3.2 | Pregman, John Jr. |
| 07/02/87 | 9 | PIM | 5 | L1.5 S | SHINING PRO | 3 | HCP | 2 | 5.1 | Blusiewicz, Leon |
| 07/05/87 | 9 | PIM | 8.5 | L1.5 | SHANGHAI SO | 3 | HCP | 2 | 11.9 | Clark, Henry S. |
| 07/06/87 | 5 | PIM | 6 | L1.5 | PRINCESS AU | 4 | C5 | 1 | 6.0 | Adams, Robert L. |
| 07/10/87 | 3 | PIM | 6 | L1.7 | FULL COTTON | 3 | C5 | 2 | 3.6 | Salzman, John Edw |
| 07/10/87 | 5 | PIM | 6 | L1.5 | BALTIMORE A | 3 | X6 | 1 | 12.1 | Cremen, Ambrose R |
| 07/11/87 | 3 | PIM | 6 | L2.5 | NORTHERN NO | 3 | X14 | 1 | 2.4 | Caviness, Thomas |
| 07/13/87 | 5 | PIM | 6 | L3 | CENTURYS' B | 3 | X6 | 2 | 4.2 | Devereux, Joseph |
| 07/17/87 | 3 | FIM | 6 | L1.5 | EXALTANT | 3 | X18 | 2 | 1.8 | Simpson, James P. |
| 07/17/87 | 6 | PIM | 6 | L3 | ENDLESS SUR | 3 | NW4 | 1 | 2.4 | Ravich, Hyman |
| 07/19/87 | 10 | PIM | 6 | L1.5 | BEMUM | 4 | C5 | 1 | 25.1 | Briones, Gaston |
| 07/14/87 | 5 | PIM | 6 | L1.5 | GRANNYETTE | 3 | X6 | 1 | 9.5 | Pruce, Ellis Y. |
| 07/14/87 | 8 | PIM | 6 | L1.7 | HAWAIIAN CO | 4 | C25 | 2 | 1.4 | Blusiewicz, Leon |
| 07/14/87 | 8 | PIM | 6 | L1.5 | LOYAL PAL | 4 | C25 | 1 | 17.8 | Kirk, Jeffrey C. |
| 07/27/87 | 9 | PIM | 8.5 | L1.5 | GRAND ROL | 3 | NW2 | 1 | 3.4 | Moncrief, Marvin |
| 01/15/87 | 3 | LRL | 6.5 | L1.5 | STUTZ PROSP | 3 | X6 | 2 | 5.5 | Moncrief, Marvin |
| 01/16/87 | 3 | LRL | 6 | L1.5 | SMART DIPLO | 3 | X18 | 1 | 3.6 | Bailes, W. Meredi |
| 01/18/87 | 2 | LRL | 6.5 | L1.5 | BOLD N DIS | 3 | C11 | 2 | 6.0 | Dinatale, John F. |
| 10/11/86 | 7 | LRL | 6 | L1.5 S | ROBERTINA | 2 | MSW | 2 | 1.0 | Delp, Gerald C. |
| 10/18/86 | 6 | LRL | 6 | L1.5 | CAPP IT OFF | 3 | HCP | 1 | 1.0 | Wilson, Gregory L |
| 10/18/86 | 8 | LRL | 10 | L1.7 S | HERAT | 3 | STK | 1 | 1.0 | Van Berg, Jack C. |
| 10/19/86 | 6 | LRL | 8.5T | L2 | ONE SISTER | 3 | C25 | 1 | 4.0 | Secor, John B. |
| 10/24/86 | 3 | LRL | 6 | L2 | COCONUT RUM | 2 | X8 | 1 | 8.1 | Salzman, John Edw |
| 10/30/86 | 6 | LRL | 6 | L3 | HAY HALO | 2 | MSW | 1 | 1.6 | Small, Richard W. |
| 12/02/86 | 6 | LRL | 7 | L2.5 | NEVER RESTL | 3 | C6 | 1 | 7.7 | Beale, Francis R. |
| 12/04/86 | 1 | LRL | 8 | L1.5 | BEAUTIFUL R | 3 | C8 | 2 | 2.1 | Leatherbury, King |
| 12/04/86 | 4 | LRL | 6 | L1.5 | MAGICAL POC | 4 | C9 | 2 | 5.3 | Leatherbury, King |
| 12/04/86 | 6 | LRL | 6 | L2 | RIGHT ROLLI | 3 | C25 | 1 | 4.6 | Moncrief, Marvin |
| 12/05/86 | 10 | LRL | 6 | L2.5 | WELL PADDED | 3 | X11 | 1 | 2.9 | Clark, Henry S. |
| 12/07/86 | 3 | LRL | 6 | L2 2TS | ELLEN'S BAB | 3 | MSW | 2 | 16.7 | Adams, Robert L. |
| 12/07/86 | 5 | LRL | 6 | L2 | CEDAR LANE | 3 | C5 | 1 | 50.3 | Nichols, Lou |
| 12/09/86 | 3 | LRL | 6 | L3.5 2TS2 | CRESTA MISS | 2 | X8 | 1 | 5.2 | Weiss, Richard |
| 12/09/86 | 10 | LRL | 6.5 | L2.5 S | HEARING AID | 3 | X6 | 1 | 3.1 | Hadry, Charles H. |
| 12/12/86 | 9 | LRL | 8.5 | L1.5 | MAJESTIC SP | 3 | C20 | 1 | 10.6 | Bullock, Alec J. |
| 12/14/86 | 8 | LRL | 8.5 | L2 | CATATONIC | 3 | NW$ | 1 | 11.1 | Leatherbury, King |

| DATE | RACE | TRK | DIST | INDEX 1 & 2 | HORSE NAME | AGE | CLASS | FIN | ODDS | TRAINER |
|------|------|-----|------|-------------|------------|-----|-------|-----|------|---------|
| 12/16/86 | 9 | LRL | 7 | L1.5 | | COUNT ON RO | 3 | C25 | 2 | 6.3 | Nanez, R. Carlos |
| 12/18/86 | 3 | LRL | 6 | L3 | | GYPSY TRADE | 2 | X14 | 2 | 3.3 | Alberts, Nancy H. |
| 12/20/86 | 2 | LRL | 8 | L1.5 | | AKUSARRE | 3 | C13 | 1 | 18.4 | Mobberley, John C |
| 12/23/86 | 2 | LRL | 8 | L1.5 | | LET'S GO TW | 3 | C5 | 1 | 4.5 | Stancer, Sandra |
| 12/29/86 | 6 | LRL | 6 | L3 | | IN A TIZZY | 2 | C14 | 1 | 6.4 | Salzman, John Edw |
| 12/29/86 | 9 | LRL | 7 | L1.5 | | APALGAFFEY | 3 | NW$ | 2 | 33.6 | Garcia, Carlos A. |
| 12/30/86 | 1 | l RL | 6 | L1.5 | | TICKA TWIST | 3 | C16 | 1 | 12.8 | Powell, Michael |
| 12/31/86 | 7 | LRL | 6 | L1.5 | | UNIVERSAL P | 3 | MSW | 2 | 92.1 | Bullock, Alec J. |
| 02/12/87 | 1 | LRL | 6 | L1.5 | | PICNIC SUPP | 4 | X14 | 2 | 25.0 | Mobberley, John C |
| 02/12/87 | 1 | LRL | 6 | L1.5 | | FRANK'S PRO | 4 | X14 | 1 | 6.8 | Schwartz, Jay |
| 02/12/87 | 6 | LRL | 8 | L1.5 | | GLOW AGAIN | 4 | C14 | 2 | 14.0 | Carton, Cheryl |
| 02/14/87 | 3 | LRL | 6 | L2 | | CHAIN GANG | 4 | C5 | 1 | 2.3 | Mullen, John P. |
| 02/14/87 | 3 | LRL | 6 | L1.5 | | WITCHELLA | 4 | C5 | 2 | 6.4 | Calvo, Frank M. |
| 02/14/87 | 4 | LRL | 6 | L1.5 | | LILLIAN P. | 4 | NW1 | 2 | 1.6 | Gaudet, Edmond D. |
| 02/14/87 | 5 | LRL | 8 | L1.5 | | OUR PATRIOT | 4 | C5 | 2 | 18.0 | Tuminelli, Joseph |
| 02/14/87 | 8 | LRL | 6 | L2.5 | | THREE RING | 3 | C25 | 2 | 7.5 | Mercer, Henry P. |
| 02/17/87 | 2 | LRL | 8.5 | L1.5 | 2TS | ALWAYS HAST | 3 | X11 | 2 | 5.9 | Robb, John J. |
| 02/16/87 | 5 | LRL | 9 | L1.5 | | DAN RATHER | 4 | C5 | 1 | 34.8 | Elliott, Janet |
| 02/16/87 | 9 | LRL | 8.5 | L1.5 | | HAY HALO | 3 | STK | 2 | 2.1 | Small, Richard W. |
| 02/19/87 | 2 | LRL | 8.5 | L1.5 | | ZEE MIMMS | 3 | MSW | 1 | 3.0 | Murphy, James W. |
| 02/19/87 | 4 | LRL | 6 | L3.5 | | CURLS AND L | 3 | X13 | 1 | 2.5 | Wheeler, David M. |
| 02/19/87 | 8 | LRL | 8.5 | L1.5 | | SOVRAN SUE | 4 | NW1 | 2 | 6.9 | Abse, Joan |
| 08/03/87 | 7 | PIM | 6 | L2.5 | 2TS2 | BLESS YOU | 2 | MSW | 1 | 6.3 | Hadry, Charles H. |
| 08/09/87 | 1 | PIM | 6 | L1.5 | | PARTYGOER | 3 | MSW | 2 | 2.0 | Anderson, Pete |
| 08/09/87 | 6 | PIM | 5 | L3 | FTT | KITCHENER'S | 3 | NW2 | 1 | 18.0 | Goswell, Michael |
| 08·18/87 | 3 | PIM | 6 | L2 | | SKATE OVER | 4 | C5 | 2 | 6.8 | Lewis, Charles R. |
| 08/18/87 | 3 | PIM | 6 | L1.5 | | MOONSHEEN | 5 | C5 | 1 | 3.3 | Campbell, Michael |
| 05/27/87 | 2 | PIM | 6 | L2 | | IRA LEE | 3 | C5 | 2 | 8.7 | Regan, Scott T. |
| 05/27/87 | 10 | PIM | 6 | L1.5 | | FACHA | 3 | X6 | 2 | 8.9 | Greene, Thomas M. |
| 08/02/87 | 7 | PIM | 5T | L3.5 | FTT | SWIFT APPEA | 3 | NW1 | 2 | 4.0 | Gaudet, Dean |
| 08/23/87 | 6 | PIM | 6 | .L1.5 | | BARE FEET | 4 | C40 | 1 | 3.2 | Tagg, Barclay |
| 08/23/87 | 7 | PIM | 8.5 | L1.5 | | GENERAL GRA | 5 | C14 | 2 | 7.4 | Allen, Harold A·. |
| 08/23/87 | 7 | PIM | 8.5 | L3.5 | | CLASSY JAY | 4 | C14 | 1 | 5.6 | Cartwright, Ronal |
| 08/07/87 | 9 | PIM | 6 | L3 | | PSYCHED | 4 | NW$ | 1 | 3.5 | Tagg, Barclay |

***** END OF FILE *****

Now that we have a list of all the WIN and PLACE finishers, we want to know if any trainers show a consistent success in this, INDEX L1-3.

**"LIST ALL NAMES THAT APPEAR ON THE ABOVE LIST 3 OR MORE TIMES."**

|                      | WINS | PLACES |
|----------------------|------|--------|
| Caviness, Thomas     | 2    | 1      |
| Clark, Henry S.      | 2    | 1      |
| Hadry, Charles H.    | 2    | 2      |
| Leatherbury, King T. | 3    | 3      |

| | | |
|---|---|---|
| Mobberley, John C. | 4 | 1 |
| Moncrief, Marvin | 3 | 1 |
| Simpson, James P. | 1 | 2 |
| Murphy, James W. | 2 | 2 |

## "SHOW US *ALL* OF THEIR ATTEMPTS, NOT JUST THE WINNERS."

| DATE | RACE | TRK | DIST | INDEX 1 & 2 | HORSE NAME | AGE | CLASS | FIN | ODDS | TRAINER |
|---|---|---|---|---|---|---|---|---|---|---|
| 05/16/87 | 10 | PIM | 8.5 | L2.5 | BOULDER TAL | 4 | C5 | 3 | 7.3 | Caviness, Thomas |
| 05/20/87 | 8 | PIM | 6 | L1.5 | MUSCOVY DUC | 3 | NW2 | 1 | 3.3 | Caviness, Thomas |
| 06/14/87 | 5 | LRL | 6 | L2 | SHARP WINGS | 3 | C18 | 7 | 3.0 | Caviness, Thomas |
| 10/07/86 | 7 | LRL | 6 | L1.5 | KAY'S LUCK | 3 | C14 | 2 | 1.4 | Caviness, Thomas |
| 07/11/87 | 3 | PIM | 6 | L2.5 | NORTHERN NO | 3 | X14 | 1 | 2.4 | Caviness, Thomas |
| 01/15/87 | 6 | LRL | 6 | L1.5 2TS | DRY STONE W | 3 | MSW | 9 | 16.9 | Caviness, Thomas |
| 04/24/87 | 6 | GS | 6 | L1.5 | FOR YOU AND | 5 | C50 | 3 | 2.0 | Caviness, Thomas |
| 08/22/87 | 3 | PHA | 6.5 | L2.5 | FOR YOU AND | 5 | C25 | 6 | 3.7 | Caviness, Thomas |
| 03/21/88 | 10 | PIM | 6 | L2 | EAGLE'S LAI | 4 | C5 | 1 | 1.2 | Caviness, Thomas |
| ***** END OF FILE ***** | | | | | | | | | | |
| 03/13/87 | 9 | LRL | 6.5 | L2 | FOOT STONE | 4 | NW3 | 1 | 2.4 | Clark, Henry S. |
| 03/20/87 | 10 | LRL | 6 | L3 | VALLEY ROAD | 3 | X11 | 9 | 34.5 | Clark, Henry S. |
| 03/23/87 | 8 | PIM | 6 | L2 | SHANGHAI SQ | 4 | NW3 | 4 | 7.0 | Clark, Henry S. |
| 07/05/87 | 9 | PIM | 8.5 | L1.5 | SHANGHAI SQ | 3 | HCP | 2 | 11.9 | Clark, Henry S. |
| 07/06/87 | 7 | PIM | 6 | L2 | DECOLLETAGE | 3 | MSW | 4 | 9.5 | Clark, Henry S. |
| 10/21/86 | 7 | LRL | 6.5 | L3 | BOZA | 3 | C18 | 8 | 49.0 | Clark, Henry S. |
| 12/05/86 | 10 | LRL | 6 | L2.5 | WELL PADDED | 3 | X11 | 1 | 2.9 | Clark, Henry S. |
| 12/09/86 | 10 | LRL | 6.5 | L1.5 2TS | VALLEY ROAD | 3 | X6 | 10 | 34.8 | Clark, Henry S. |
| ***** END OF FILE ***** | | | | | | | | | | |

| DATE | RACE | TRK | DIST | INDEX 1 & 2 | | HORSE NAME | AGE | CLASS | FIN | ODDS | TRAINER |
|------|------|-----|------|-------------|--|------------|-----|-------|-----|------|---------|
| 03/10/87 | 8 | LRL | 6 | L2 | | BAL DU BOIS | 3 | NW2 | 1 | 19.2 | Hadry, Charles H. |
| 03/12/87 | 9 | LRL | 6.5 | L2.5 | | BALLOON MEE | 4 | C18 | 6 | 6.7 | Hadry, Charles H. |
| 03/13/87 | 5 | LRL | 6 | L2 | | HIS REVEREN | 3 | X30 | 9 | 57.0 | Hadry, Charles H. |
| 03/17/87 | 9 | LRL | 6.5 | L2.5 | | DOVER RIDGE | 4 | C50 | 1 | 1.4 | Hadry, Charles H. |
| 05/21/87 | 8 | PIM | 6 | L1.5 | | NORLAND NAN | 3 | NW2 | 2 | 5.6 | Hadry, Charles H. |
| 06/01/87 | 9 | LRL | 8.5 | L1.5 | | JUSAVIK | 4 | C25 | 2 | 1.1 | Hadry, Charles H. |
| 06/08/87 | 10 | LRL | 6 | L1.7 | | MERRY ACTOR | 3 | X6 | 5 | 3.1 | Hadry, Charles H. |
| 11/13/86 | 3 | LRL | 7 | L2.5 | S | NOBLE STATE | 3 | MSW | 6 | 5.3 | Hadry, Charles H. |
| 01/19/87 | 3 | LRL | 6 | L1.5 | | HEARING AID | 4 | C5 | 3 | 5.1 | Hadry, Charles H. |
| 10/17/86 | 8 | LRL | 8 | L1.7 | | NEAR EAST | 3 | C25 | 4 | 2.7 | Hadry, Charles H. |
| 12/09/86 | 10 | LRL | 6.5 | L2.5 | S | HEARING AID | 3 | X6 | 1 | 3.1 | Hadry, Charles H. |
| 02/14/87 | 9 | LRL | 9 | L1.5 | | FINDER'S RE | 4 | HCP | 4 | 8.3 | Hadry, Charles H. |
| 08/03/87 | 7 | PIM | 6 | L2.5 | 2TS2 | BLESS YOU | 2 | MSW | 1 | 6.3 | Hadry, Charles H. |

***** END OF FILE *****

| DATE | RACE | TRK | DIST | INDEX 1 & 2 | | HORSE NAME | AGE | CLASS | FIN | ODDS | TRAINER |
|------|------|-----|------|-------------|--|------------|-----|-------|-----|------|---------|
| 03/10/87 | 4 | LRL | 6 | L2 | | PARTIDA | 3 | X30 | 7 | 1.9 | Leatherbury, King |
| 03/13/87 | 8 | LRL | 8.5 | L2 | | CHIC WEED | 4 | C14 | 1 | 2.5 | Leatherbury, King |
| 04/06/87 | 5 | PIM | 9 | L3 | | EDGAR'S GIR | 4 | C5 | 1 | 1.5 | Leatherbury, King |
| 05/02/87 | 9 | PIM | 8T | L2 | 2TT | WISKERS SAI | 3 | STK | 10 | 35.6 | Leatherbury, King |
| 05/05/87 | 4 | PIM | 8.5 | L1.5 | | LING LING | 4 | C14 | 4 | 2.0 | Leatherbury, King |
| 05/05/87 | 8 | PIM | 8.5 | L1.5 | | THAT'LL BE | 3 | NW1 | 4 | 26.0 | Leatherbury, King |
| 06/25/87 | 10 | LRL | 6.5 | L3 | | ESPIRIT DE | 4 | C11 | 3 | 3.2 | Leatherbury, King |
| 10/07/86 | 9 | LRL | 8 | L1.7 | | CHIC WEED | 4 | C9 | 3 | 1.7 | Leatherbury, King |
| 12/29/86 | 4 | LRL | 8 | L2.5 | | HEUBETCHACA | 4 | C8 | 2 | 3.0 | Leatherbury, King |
| 07/11/87 | 4 | PIM | 6 | L1.5 | | NOBLE BUT N | 4 | C35 | 5 | 3.1 | Leatherbury, King |
| 07/13/87 | 8 | PIM | 6 | L1.7 | | DRAT FOOT | 4 | C25 | 4 | 1.9 | Leatherbury, King |
| 07/18/87 | 4 | PIM | 6 | L1.5 | | CONFIDED | 4 | C11 | 4 | 4.0 | Leatherbury, King |
| 10/18/86 | 5 | LRL | 6 | L3.5 | | HOPE ME DIE | 3 | HCP | 10 | 60.2 | Leatherbury, King |
| 12/04/86 | 1 | LRL | 8 | L1.5 | | BEAUTIFUL R | 3 | C8 | 2 | 2.1 | Leatherbury, King |
| 12/04/86 | 4 | LRL | 6 | L1.5 | | MAGICAL POC | 4 | C9 | 2 | 5.3 | Leatherbury, King |
| 12/04/86 | 5 | LRL | 6.5 | L3.5 | | WOLF CALL I | 3 | C5 | 4 | 21.8 | Leatherbury, King |
| 12/14/86 | 8 | LRL | 8.5 | L2 | | CATATONIC | 3 | NW$ | 1 | 11.1 | Leatherbury, King |
| 12/27/86 | 5 | LRL | 6 | L1.5 | | PARTIDA | 2 | MSW | 3 | 23.0 | Leatherbury, King |
| 12/27/86 | 9 | LRL | 10 | L1.5 | | BRILLIANT S | 3 | HCP | 5 | 14.4 | Leatherbury, King |
| 09/29/86 | 9 | BEL | 6 | L2 | 2TS | CROOKED | 3 | MSW | 8 | 6.1 | Leatherbury, King |
| 02/13/87 | 4 | LRL | 8.5 | L1.5 | | MINI DON | 4 | C11 | 4 | 7.2 | Leatherbury, King |
| 05/10/87 | 6 | BEL | 6 | L2 | | CROOKED | 4 | NW2 | 3 | 4.7 | Leatherbury, King |

***** END OF FILE *****

| DATE | RACE | TRK | DIST | INDEX 1 & 2 | | HORSE NAME | AGE | CLASS | FIN | ODDS | TRAINER |
|------|------|-----|------|-------------|--|------------|-----|-------|-----|------|---------|
| 03/26/87 | 8 | PIM | 8.5 | L1.5 | | BAS DU BEBE | 4 | NW2 | 3 | 10.9 | Murphy, James W. |
| 05/14/87 | 7 | PIM | 6 | L1.5 | | SHEBEEN | 3 | C6 | 2 | 7.3 | Murphy, James W. |
| 05/22/87 | 6 | PIM | 6 | L1.5 | S | WHAT'S DIS | 3 | X30 | 3 | 5.5 | Murphy, James W. |
| 05/23/87 | 8 | PIM | 8.5 | L1.5 | | FORTUNATE F | 3 | NW1 | 5 | 2.2 | Murphy, James W. |
| 06/08/87 | 8 | LRL | 8.5T | L2.5 | S | CHRISTIANA | 3 | NW2 | 1 | 5.0 | Murphy, James W. |
| 10/03/86 | 7 | LRL | 8.5T | L1.5 | | DARBRIELLE | 4 | NW$ | 2 | 1.7 | Murphy, James W. |
| 10/03/86 | 9 | LRL | 8 | L2 | | HELLO HEART | 3 | HCP | 4 | 12.6 | Murphy, James W. |
| 10/09/86 | 8 | LRL | 6 | L2 | | NORTH OF DA | 3 | NW1 | 3 | 7.5 | Murphy, James W. |
| 07/11/87 | 4 | PIM | 6 | L2 | | SMARTEN UP | 4 | C35 | 6 | 6.3 | Murphy, James W. |
| 10/17/86 | 6 | LRL | 7 | L1.5 | | L'ENJEREE | 2 | X25 | 7 | 4.5 | Murphy, James W. |
| 10/19/86 | 5 | LRL | 8.5T | L2 | | SARATOGA GO | 3 | MSW | 12 | 17.5 | Murphy, James W. |
| 12/31/86 | 7 | LRL | 6 | L1.5 | | NO HESITATI | 3 | MSW | 8 | 47.1 | Murphy, James W. |
| 02/19/87 | 2 | LRL | 8.5 | L1.5 | | ZEE MIMMS | 3 | MSW | 1 | 3.0 | Murphy, James W. |

***** END OF FILE *****

| DATE | RACE | TRK | DIST | INDEX 1 & 2 | | HORSE NAME | AGE | CLASS | FIN | ODDS | TRAINER |
|------|------|-----|------|-------------|---|------------|-----|-------|-----|------|---------|
| 03/27/86 | 9 | PIM | 9 | L1.5 | | SCOTCH HEAT | 4 | NW$ | 1 | 5.6 | Mobberley, John C |
| 04/14/87 | 8 | PIM | 8.5 | L1.5 | | PLATINUM FO | 4 | C25 | 10 | 18.1 | Mobberley, John C |
| 05/18/87 | 9 | PIM | 6 | L1.5 | | BROADWAY BI | 3 | NW4 | 6 | 10.2 | Mobberley, John C |
| 01/01/87 | 1 | LRL | 6.5 | L1.5 | | BANNER YET | 5 | C8 | 1 | 7.0 | Mobberley, John C |
| 05/25/87 | 8 | PIM | 6 | L2 | | FAST MEMORY | 3 | NW$ | 7 | 45.8 | Mobberley, John C |
| 11/11/86 | 6 | LRL | 6.5 | L1.5 | | BANNER YET | 3 | C6 | 1 | 8.7 | Mobberley, John C |
| 07/11/87 | 4 | PIM | 6 | L1.5 | | BROADWAY BI | 4 | C35 | 7 | 26.1 | Mobberley, John C |
| 07/20/87 | 9 | PIM | 8.5T | L1.5 | | FAST MEMORY | 3 | NW$ | 7 | 20.7 | Mobberley, John C |
| 10/26/86 | 1 | LRL | 8 | L3 | | JOLLY PEG | 3 | C25 | 3 | 5.8 | Mobberley, John C |
| 12/20/86 | 2 | LRL | 8 | L1.5 | | AKUSARRE | 3 | C13 | 1 | 18.4 | Mobberley, John C |
| 02/12/87 | 1 | LRL | 6 | L1.5 | | PICNIC SUPP | 4 | X14 | 2 | 25.0 | Mobberley, John C |
| ***** END OF FILE ***** | | | | | | | | | | | |
| | | | | | | | | | | | |
| 09/12/86 | 8 | BEL | 7T | L2 | S | LISA LEIGH | 3 | STK | 11 | 35.7 | Moncrief, Marvin |
| 03/06/87 | 2 | LRL | 6 | L1.5 | | RAINBOW LAS | 4 | MSW | 5 | 18.1 | Moncrief, Marvin |
| 03/12/87 | 4 | LRL | 6 | L2.5 | | SUGAR N CRE | 3 | NW2 | 4 | 2.7 | Moncrief, Marvin |
| 03/23/87 | 10 | PIM | 6 | L2.5 | | MAGICAL TUN | 3 | X30 | 11 | 9.4 | Moncrief, Marvin |
| 03/27/86 | 6 | PIM | 8.5 | L1.5 | | EXSABLE | 4 | C35 | 6 | 27.0 | Moncrief, Marvin |
| 05/05/87 | 1 | PIM | 8.5 | L1.5 | | STUTZ PROSP | 3 | C5 | 5 | 4.3 | Moncrief, Marvin |
| 06/23/87 | 10 | LRL | 7 | L1.7 | | RAINBOW LAS | 3 | X11 | 3 | 1.4 | Moncrief, Marvin |
| 01/05/87 | 7 | LRL | 6 | L2 | | ROLLICKING | 4 | C6 | 10 | 20.9 | Moncrief, Marvin |
| 07/27/87 | 9 | PIM | 8.5 | L1.5 | | GRAND ROL | 3 | NW2 | 1 | 3.4 | Moncrief, Marvin |
| 01/15/87 | 3 | LRL | 6.5 | L1.5 | | STUTZ PROSP | 3 | X6 | 2 | 5.5 | Moncrief, Marvin |
| 10/21/86 | 4 | LRL | 6 | L1.5 | 2TS2 | STUTZ PROSP | 2 | X11 | 7 | 6.0 | Moncrief, Marvin |
| 12/04/86 | 6 | LRL | 6 | L2 | | RIGHT ROLLI | 3 | C25 | 1 | 4.6 | Moncrief, Marvin |
| 12/26/86 | 6 | LRL | 6.5 | L1.5 | | SUGAR N CRE | 2 | STK | 6 | 4.3 | Moncrief, Marvin |
| 01/09/86 | 11 | GP | 8.5 | L2 | S | LISA LEIGH | 4 | NW3 | 10 | 8.0 | Moncrief, Marvin |
| 01/22/86 | 11 | GP | 7 | L1.5 | S | TROPICAL WH | 3 | NW$ | 13 | 14.0 | Moncrief, Marvin |
| 01/31/86 | 9 | GP | 7 | L3 | S | DON'S CHOIC | 4 | HCP | 2 | 2.0 | Moncrief, Marvin |
| 02/05/86 | 6 | GP | 6 | L3 | S | EDWIN MOSES | 3 | C35 | 6 | 45.0 | Moncrief, Marvin |
| 08/06/87 | 9 | SAR | 5 | L2.5 | | CLEVER POWE | 2 | MSW | 1 | 2.7 | Moncrief, Marvin |
| ***** END OF FILE ***** | | | | | | | | | | | |
| | | | | | | | | | | | |
| 03/21/87 | 10 | LRL | 6.5 | L1.5 | | BLUE AND BO | 3 | X6 | 1 | 3.6 | Simpson, James P. |
| 03/25/87 | 4 | PIM | 6 | L2.5 | | ABSURD BIRD | 4 | C35 | 4 | 6.9 | Simpson, James P. |
| 04/03/87 | 4 | PIM | 6 | L2.5 | | THESPIS | 3 | C30 | 2 | 5.9 | Simpson, James P. |
| 05/05/87 | 10 | PIM | 6 | L2 | S | LORDS A LEA | 3 | X8 | 6 | 17.7 | Simpson, James P. |
| 06/02/87 | 2 | LRL | 6 | L1.5 | | EXALTANT | 3 | X25 | 4 | 1.1 | Simpson, James P. |
| 10/07/86 | 7 | LRL | 6 | L2 | | SMART TALKE | 3 | C14 | 3 | 6.2 | Simpson, James P. |
| 07/02/87 | 8 | PIM | 6 | L1.5 | | FINE WIND | 3 | NW2 | 6 | 5.0 | Simpson, James P. |
| 07/17/87 | 3 | PIM | 6 | L1.5 | | EXALTANT | 3 | X18 | 2 | 1.8 | Simpson, James P. |
| ***** END OF FILE ***** | | | | | | | | | | | |

DO ANY OF THE ABOVE TRAINERS SHOW A NET
PROFIT OF 150% OR MORE IN THIS INDEX ACTIVITY?"

| Trainer +/- | Cost | Win 1 | Win 2 | Win 3 | Win 4 | Net % |
|---|---|---|---|---|---|---|
| Cav'ness | $18 | 8.60 | 6.80 | 4.40 | | + 10% |
| Clark | $16 | 6.80 | 7.80 | | | - 9% |
| Hadry | $26 | 40.40 | 4.80 | 8.20 | 14.60 | +162% |
| Lea'bury | $44 | 7.00 | 5.00 | 24.20 | | - 18% |
| Mob'rley | $22 | 13.20 | 16.00 | 19.40 | 38.80 | +297% |
| Moncrief | $36 | 8.80 | 11.20 | 7.40 | | - 24% |
| Simpson | $16 | 9.20 | | | | - 42% |
| Murphy | $26 | 12.00 | 8.00 | | | - 30% |

There's no question about one of these trainers offering a great
opportunity. Hadry, showing 162% looks good on the surface,
but he got most of this on one, big win. John Mobberley is the
man. Let's look at his races in chronological order and try to
determine at what point (if any) he was worth a beginning bet.

| | | | | |
|---|---|---|---|---|
| 03/27/86 | 1 | $ 5.60 | 05/18/87 | 6th |
| 10/26/86 | 3rd | | 05/25/87 | 7th |
| 11/11/86 | 1 | 8.70 | 07/11/87 | 7th |
| 12/20/86 | 1 | 19.40 | 07/20/87 | 7th |
| 01/10/87 | 1 | 7.00 | end | |
| 04/14/87 | 10th | | | |

Mr. Mobberley shows a definite talent for INDEX L1-3.
Examining his complete record with all INDEX RUNNERS we
learn he has something else to offer, also. Examine his "Rt7".

```
                         Trainer  Record  File
```

| | | | | | | | | | | | |
|---|---|---|---|---|---|---|---|---|---|---|---|
| 01/01/87 | 1 | LRL 6.5 | L1.5 | | BANNER YET | 5 | C8 | 1 | 7.0 | Mobberley, | John C |
| 02/12/87 | 1 | LRL 6 | L1.5 | | PICNIC SUPP | 4 | X14 | 2 | 25.0 | Mobberley, | John C |
| 03/27/86 | 9 | PIM 9 | L1.5 | | SCOTCH HEAT | 4 | NW$ | 1 | 5.6 | Mobberley, | John C |
| 04./14/87 | 8 | PIM 8.5 | L1.5 | | PLATINUM FO | 4 | C25 | 10 | 18.1 | Mobberley, | John C |
| 05/18/87 | 9 | PIM 6 | L1.5 | | BROADWAY BI | 3 | NW4 | 6 | 10.2 | Mobberley, | John C |
| 05/25/87 | 8 | PIM 6 | L2 | | FAST MEMORY | 3 | NW$ | 7 | 45.8 | Mobberley, | John C |
| 06/07/87 | 4 | LRL 8.5T | 2L2 | | FAST MEMORY | 3 | NW$ | 6 | 13.8 | Mobberley, | John C |
| 06/25/87 | 5 | LRL 6 | PTS | | QUIET RETRE | 3 | X8 | 9 | 19.1 | Mobberley, | John C |
| 06/28/87 | 4 | LRL 6.5 | FTS | | LORDIE MISS | 3 | X30 | 6 | 3.9 | Mobberley, | John C |
| 06/30/87 | 6 | LRL 6.5 | 2L1. | | NATIONAL RE | 3 | C1ɔ | 5 | 4.2 | Mobberley, | John C |
| 07/05/87 | 3 | PIM 6 | FTS | | HUCKLEBERRY | 3 | MSW | 8 | 12.8 | Mobberley, | John C |
| 07/11/87 | 2 | PIM 8.5 | 2TS | | LORDIE MISS | 3 | MSW | 7 | 12.7 | Mobberley, | John C |
| 07/11/87 | 4 | PIM 6 | L1.5 | | BROADWAY BI | 4 | C35 | 7 | 26.1 | Mobberley, | John C |
| 07/20/87 | 9 | PIM 8.5T | L1.5 | | FAST MEMORY | 3 | NW$ | 7 | 20.7 | Mobberley, | John C |
| 08/03/87 | 9 | PIM 6 | 2L1. | | BROADWAY BI | 4 | NW$ | 6 | 14.0 | Mobberley, | John C |
| 08/09/87 | 8 | PIM 8 | FTT | StR | BANNER YET | 5 | NW2 | 8 | 19.0 | Mobberley, | John C |
| 08/17/87 | 7 | PIM 8.5 | FTT | | HUCKLEBERRY | 3 | MSW | 8 | 13.0 | Mobberley, | John C |
| 10/03/87 | 6 | PIM 8.5 | L2 | | PLATINUM FO | 5 | C18 | 1 | 3.9 | Mobberley, | John C |
| 10/16/86 | 8 | LRL 7 | Rt7 | | FUR COLLAR | 3 | C25 | 7 | 6.3 | Mobberley, | John C |
| 10/19/86 | 5 | LRL 8.5T | FTT | | PURE PURPLE | 3 | MSW | 4 | 16.3 | Mobberley, | John C |
| 10/26/86 | 1 | LRL 8 | L3 | | JOLLY PEG | 3 | C25 | 3 | 5.8 | Mobberley, | John C |
| 11/11/86 | 6 | LRL 6.5 | L1.5 | | BANNER YET | 3 | C6 | 1 | 8.7 | Mobberley, | John C |
| 11/22/86 | 3 | LRL 7 | Rt7 | | DOUBLE STIT | 3 | C30 | 1 | 6.7 | Mobberley, | John C |
| 11/27/86 | 3 | LRL 7 | L4 | | NIGHT AHEAD | 3 | MSW | 6 | 21.4 | Mobberley, | John C |
| 12/04/86 | 8 | LRL 7 | Rt7 | FBK | FAST MEMORY | 3 | NW3 | 1 | 3.5 | Mobberley, | John C |
| 12/05/86 | 10 | LRL 6 | 2L4 | | NIGHT AHEAD | 3 | X11 | 2 | 3.2 | Mobberley, | John C |
| 12/14/86 | 9 | LRL 7 | Rt7 | | MIDNIGHT CA | 3 | STK | 2 | .8 | Mobberley, | John C |
| 12/20/86 | 10 | LRL 8T | 2TT | | PURE PURPLE | 3 | MSW | 2 | 6.0 | Mobberley, | John C |
| 12/20/86 | 2 | LRL 8 | L1.5 | | AKUSARRE | 3 | C13 | 1 | 18.4 | Mobberley, | John C |
| 10/09/86 | 4 | LRL 8 | STR | | GOLD SPOON | 3 | C5 | 6 | 10.3 | Mobberley, | JOhn C |

Questions even more complex are no problem if the detail bits and pieces are somewhere in the memory bank. You can't get an answer unless you've gone to the painstaking trouble of putting the data in; and this is the bottom line on "why" trainer handicapping will enjoy an untroubled romp for many, many years.

Another useful computer program compiles statistical data as each single record is added. It creates "balances" in both dollars and cents (calculated on a $2 bet), and in net profit percent (+/), cumulative from 1985 for every trainer, in every Index carried.

Toggling through this file, trainer by trainer, you can see such things as:

FTS          + $274.00          + 1,666% (net)

This is always an attention-getter. When going into this trainer's record of details, one can find that he earned these incredible totals in the way similar to Charles Hadry in the search above; putting over one longshot in many tries. There's no denying the profit but that isn't the kind of performance we're seeking.

Nineteen out of twenty turn out to be useless; but that still leaves one.

Eventually, going through today's *Racing Form* became a problem. The names of all the trainers who have a profitable Index going on the east coast are in my head, but I lose track of some Index and some conditions attached to the Index. This list keeps growing and it's easy to overlook an opportunity.

The logical procedure gave birth to a file containing all those names, Index and conditions. After the paper is coded, the Index Runners are entered immediately. A few keystrokes after that sets up a search through that file to see if any of today's names, Index and conditions match up. In seconds, a printout of every opportunity running today in the east can be completed. It doesn't forget.

The miracles a PC can perform with complicated search criteria are too numerous to detail here. Beginning this job without one was a matter of ignorance on my part, costing time, money and efficiency.

Remember that bottom line on why trainer handicapping will enjoy an untroubled romp for many years... it's too damn much work for most.

Begin now. You'll still be among the first.

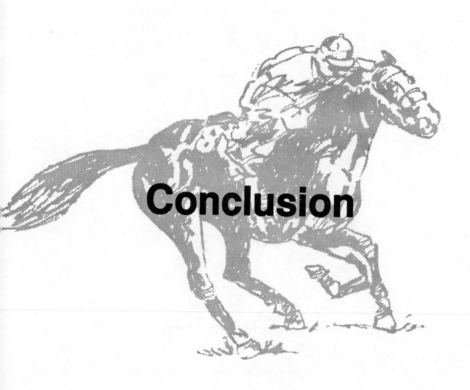

# Conclusion

# Conclusion

The method of investing in trainers as described in this book may assume forbidding proportions. Clearly, for those who are unwilling to do the enormous amount of work involved, handicapping trainers may be limited in its application.

But before chucking this into a corner, reconsider two matters that might have become buried in details.

Number One: The only purpose from the beginning of the project through and beyond the last proofs of validity, was to help the author cash more tickets of greater value. He was a horseplayer who wanted to make more money. It was a very personal thing. If he could have found the button marked "Instant Riches," he would have leaned on it.

Immediately following the decision to go, came the questions where, and how? It was uncharted territory. There was a need to waste huge blocks of time and trouble discovering and sorting what was relevant from what was not. A lot of work went into a very small beginning and, as a result, the territory is now charted for anybody who wants to follow.

Begin anywhere, with a single trainer or track, with an Index. Choose one or more and go from there. Wisdom suggests a small and cautious beginning regardless of how much is known or believed or how many dollars one is prepared to plunge.

Number Two: The author abandoned his "one track smooth-running machine" (wherein he doubled his original bankroll three-and-one-half times in the first six months) to pursue the much larger project of creating a nationwide database that did not exist at the time. After the parameters were well established, he could have kept it simple. He deliberately chose to complicate his life; multiply his workload.

To begin, one may choose a trainer and Index mentioned in these pages. They are likely to be still profitable but as more and more followers climb aboard, the point of diminishing returns approaches rapidly. The author does not recommend this and not because of the money.

Searching memory for the most satisfying event of his experience with handicapping trainers, nothing compares with the recollection of "OK Fine" stretching out his lead on the Hialeah homestretch that Spring afternoon. "OK Fine" was the first. The author freely admits he does not have the talent to convey the incredible joy of that experience in these pages. He would never do it if he could; preferring to leave it on the table for any who might choose to pick it up -- the joy of discovery.

# Glossary

# Glossary

ALPHABETIZER: Step #2 (follows coding) when collecting data by hand (no computer). Used to line up trainer names by alphabet letter to facilitate easy entry on the individual trainer record.

BOX BET (TRIPLE): "Box A and B and All." A multi-combination trifecta bet used when there are two horses expected to finish in the money. Boxing these two with all others in the race assures a payoff if the chosen two finish in the money, regardless of the order.

BULLRING: A racetrack of 6 furlongs or less in total distance.

CLAIMING RACE: Any race wherein a properly licensed person may seize ownership of any horse entered by:

1) Posting the listed price with the Racing Secretary prior to the running and,

2) Being the first qualified to do so. Where more than one claim slip is entered for a single horse, some tracks will hold a second drawing. Ownership is transferred by the bell opening the starting gate. Any purse monies won by the claimed horse belong to the owner who entered the horse in the race. If the horse breaks down during the running of the race, it is the responsibility of the new owner to see to all appropriate details.

CODING: Step #1 in any data collecting operation. The process of identifying and marking (in the *Daily Racing Form*) all horses that are entered under one or more of the situations chosen for study.

EXACTA (PERFECTA): A bet that requires a bettor to predict the exact order in which the first two horses will cross the finish line.

EXOTIC: A name given to ANY bet other than WIN, PLACE or SHOW. Daily Double, Exacta, Trifecta, Super Six, Twin Triple, Quinella, etc., are all exotic bets.

FURLONG: 1/8th (0.125) of one mile.

HIGH-VISIBILITY: A situation "result" that may become evident simply by reading the *Daily Racing Form*. First and Second Time Starters, Claimed horses, First Time Turf runners, Imported horses, Blinker options, Up or Down in Class, etc., are all high-visibility situations.

IN JAIL: The period of 30 days following the claim of a horse is the time the horse is said to be "In Jail." If the trainer chooses to run the horse during this period, the first race after the claim must be in a class at least 25% higher than the class of the race from which the horse was claimed.

MARTINGALE: A gambling method that requires a systematic change in the bet after wins or losses.

ROUTE: Generally, a race that is run around two turns of a standard, mile-oval track. Knowledgeable students of pace consider a mile race to be the longest of the sprints. However, traditionally, races that are one mile or longer are referred to as routes. Tracks of extreme proportions (Belmont Park and Sportsman's Park) require a more precise description.

SPRINT: A race that is not a Route (see above). Generally, 7.5 furlongs or less, run in a straight line or around only one turn.

TRIFECTA (TRIPLE): A bet that requires a bettor to predict the exact order in which the first three horses will cross the finish line.

# Acknowledgments

The following list of items, Copyright (1987) DAILY RACING FORM, INC. are reprinted with permission of the copyright owner.

| Item 1 - | 12/31/85 | 6 Crc | Past Performances | Page 38 |
| Item 2 - | 4/15/86 | 8 Hia | Past Performances | 58 |
| Item 3 - | 4/15/86 | 8 Hia | Result Chart | 59 |
| Item 4 - | 4/15/86 | 9 Hia | Past Performances | 60 |
| Item 5 - | 4/15/86 | 9 Hia | Result Chart | 61 |
| Item 6 - | 4/16/86 | 6 Hia | Past Performances | 61 |
| Item 7 - | 4/16/86 | 6 Hia | Result Chart | 62 |
| Item 8 - | 8/29/86 | 1 Crc | Past Performances, Listings, Selections | 91 |
| Item 9 - | 8/29/86 | 1 Crc | Result Chart | 93 |

# PUBLISHER'S ADDENDUM

Liberty Publishing Company, Inc. is now one of the leading publishers and distributors of horse racing books and software. These and other LPC titles are available at better bookstores everywhere or may be ordered directly from the publisher...

WINNING AT THE TRACK by David L. Christopher, offers a fast, easy and reliable handicapping method. "If you enjoy going to the track, you cannot afford to be without this book!" (*The Backstretch* Magazine) $9.95  160 pages

WINNING AT THE TRACK Software is easily the best racing program available at any price. The software can correct to all of the major North American track surfaces, dirt or turf, and features a parallel speed table to automatically adjust the distances of each horse's past performances. Includes 160-page book. $49.95 (5 1/4" disc) $69.95 (3 1/2" disc)

FAST AND FIT HORSES  Bob Heyburn's classic book on *pace* and *form* is now in paperback for the first time. $9.95 160 pages

THE MATHEMATICS OF HORSE RACING by David B. Fogel, should be owned by every serious fan of thoroughbred racing. This new guide answers questions that "speed" and "class" handicappers have asked for years. $9.95  144 pages

TEN STEPS TO WINNING by Danny Holmes offers a professional handicapping method that anyone can use. $9.95  160 pages

Other books available from Liberty Publishing Company...

TOTAL VICTORY AT THE TRACK by William Scott  $12.95

HOW WILL YOUR HORSE RUN TODAY? by William L. Scott  $9.95

HORSES TALK:  IT PAYS TO LISTEN by Trillis Parker  $19.95

THE COMPLETE GUIDE TO RACETRACK BETTING by D. Rosenthal  $9.95

To:  **Liberty Publishing Company, Inc.**
440 South Federal Highway - Suite 202
Deerfield Beach, Florida  33441
(305) 360-9000

### ORDER FORM

- - - - - - - - - - - - - - - - - - - - - - - - - - - - - - - - - - - - - - - - - - - - - - - - - - - -

Gentlemen:

Please rush the following order to the address noted below. Enclosed is my check for $_____ which includes the retail price of the title(s) noted plus $2.00 for shipping and handling.

| Qty. | Title |
| --- | --- |
| _____ | _____ |
| _____ | _____ |
| _____ | _____ |
| _____ | _____ |
| _____ | _____ |

Ship to: _____
(Name)

_____
(Street)

_____
(City, State and Zip)